To Lois,
I am so pleased to send you a copy of my book. If only I had been a writer back when you and Deb House-sat. What a trip that was!

George Bellem

Lois, Hope you enjoy reading about our adventures.

Bob Gurin

The Beldens Go To......

The Strange Adventures of Three Not Quite Normal People From Ohio

By

George Belden

Tripnavvy Press
Kent, Ohio

Also by George Belden

The Windham Bombers:
The First Half Century of Small Town Athletics

First Edition

ISBN-13: 978-1544627014

ISBN-10: 1544627017

To Helena and Bob:

May our odyssey never end.

Introduction

I'm not sure why you are reading this book. If you have encountered George Belden at any point in his seven decades on earth, you are aware that he is an unprincipled liar and you know full well what is coming.

If, however, you have never had the pleasure of his company, every single word you are about to read is the gospel truth, as he understands the term.

The two main characters in this tome, George and Helena Belden, have been together since the age of six. They are graduates of the very small school system of Windham, Ohio, and were in the same classroom from second grade on. Their first date was their junior/senior prom, and they were married three years later. In every possible way, they are joined at the hip. They are also both quite bizarre, and happy to be so.

George began writing in sixth grade; his first story was "Joe and George in the Belden Congo." He taught English for 30 years at Maple Heights High School, including Television Journalism, Studies In Popular Culture, Literature of Sports, and British Literature. He coached football, and was the head coach of both volleyball and golf.

Helena never escaped the clutches of Windham, and spent 30 years teaching fourth grade in the very school in which she had been educated. She also became a nationally known quilter.

As they neared retirement, they decided to become world travelers, midwestern innocents abroad, and George began writing about their adventures and mishaps and sending those missives to the few people who would admit to being his friend. Later sojourns coincided with the growth of the internet and technology; the earlier trips were brief observations hammered out at internet cafes which charged an exorbitant rate per minute. Later, he took a laptop on trips and was able to take advantage of the growth of WiFi hotspots, so his scribblings became more immediate and extensive.

This book is the "best" of his efforts, although since you paid your money, you get to decide.

The reader will notice distinct stylistic variations. The first two chapters, The Beldens Go To Iceland and Bermuda, are the last pieces George has written. The second part of the book begins with the earliest trip to England, and then moves forward in time. Be patient – the 2000 trip was his baby steps; he becomes a different (hopefully better) writer with every voyage. Language snobs be warned; some chapters are in first person, some are in third person, and second person even rears its ugly head occasionally.

About halfway through the book, a third character joins George and Helena in their travels. Bob Geiser coached football with George and they have been best friends since. Bob taught social studies, became an athletic director, and eventually went into school administration. He is a widower, and when he retired, he became the companion on many of the Beldens' trips. In fact, the trio takes an annual fall golf trip that is both invigorating and exhausting. Bob's personality quirks are what makes him so endearing. And he is crazy enough to actually allow this book to appear without any editorial control.

So now you have the background. I've got quite a story to tell you. In fact, I can't wait to hear it myself...

The Beldens Go To Iceland 2015

So how did George Allen Belden, a simple lad from Windham Ohio, and Helena Fatima Belden, born in a chicken coop in Gundernhausen Germany, come to be standing in the middle of a street in Reykjavik, Iceland, snot running from their noses, unable to see more than three feet in front of themselves because of the tears clouding their eyes due to the wind howling at 40 mph to go with the 28 degree temperature and snow pelting them, wearing fancy ICELAND logo hats they had just paid 2500 Króna each for because neither of them thought to pack earmuffs for the trip, and trying to decide if this would be a nice day for whale watching?

Funny you should ask. It's a story too long to tell in one sitting. But it has to start somewhere.

That would be last October, the day before George's 65th birthday, back when he was young enough to still possess some common sense. He was sitting at his computer, shuffling through the multitude of "deal of the century" Groupons that flow through his Gmail account, when one caught his attention. An airline he had never heard of: WOW. That's its name, not a description: WOW. It was a brand new budget startup airline, based in Iceland, and as a come-on for the first people foolhardy enough to trust them, it was offering round-trip flights from Boston to Reykjavik for little more than George spends on golf every week during the summer.

Never thinking she would say yes, George yelled at Helena, "Hey, how would you like to go to Iceland?"

She said sure.

Oh, shit.

When Helena decides to do something, she dedicates her whole life to it. For the next four months, nothing existed except planning for Iceland. Can you cook dinner? No, there's this visa form that I just have to get done today - it's only three more months until we leave. Should we pay the extra $25 each for two more inches of leg room? Do you think we can fly five hours without going to the bathroom - we can save $3 each if we can hold it. Folks, this woman researched everything about this budget airline down to the last farthing.

She has a friend in her Silver Sneakers aerobics class that has been to Iceland many times, and he filled her with stories of the wondrous natural sights they would see, and gave her brochures that showed smiling Scandinavian beauties swimming half-nude in geothermal pools, which of course she hid from George because she didn't want him to have a heart attack before departure, since the airfare was non-refundable. What her Silver Sneakers friend didn't show her were the tragic people eaten by polar bears attracted by the stench of putrid shark meat, the Icelandic national dish, on their breath. Or that the geothermal pools reek of sulfur, so those pulchritudinous blondes in the brochure also smell like they just farted in a very small elevator.

But no matter. Helena was committed to this venture, and her days were filled with combing through the splendors of various Reykjavik hotels, sifting their descriptions until she could find the very best, most comfortable, most centrally located one. She never once remembered that since these are EUROPEAN hotels, the rooms are smaller than that elevator the blondes were farting in. That the bathrooms are so tiny you have to sit sideways on the toilet and hope that the important part got centered and wasn't hanging out over one of the edges. That the beds are so narrow that your legs hang over each side. That there is no word for "comfort" in the Icelandic language. Not remembering ANY of these things, Helena followed the guidance of her Holy Bible, aka TripAdvisor, and booked us into the Hotel Foss Lind.

And George's few friends, the people who constantly lure him onto the golf course only to siphon mounds of cash out of his pocket by playing for blood money, told him, "You can't go to Iceland and not play golf. It's the chance of a lifetime!" So George spent the entirety of the most miserable Ohio winter on record dreaming of going to the country which has more golf courses per capita than any other nation on earth. As Aerosmith once sang, "Dream on."

As the dreadful winter gave way to 35 degree April days balmy enough to put on five layers of clothes and go smite the ball at the Oak Knolls golf course, Helena and George, both entertained with visions of exotic adventures near the Arctic Circle, consulted the online Weather Channel to decide what to pack for the trip.

Weather people are the biggest bullshitters on earth...but more on that tomorrow.

Part 2

WOW Airlines allows one piece of luggage weighing 40 pounds, for which one pays $130. Hell, George's underpants for one week weigh 40 pounds, so he contemplated going commando, Viking style, while Helena said that we could buy a whole new wardrobe for that much and we should go empty-handed. But in the end they caved, buying all the extras, including $5 if they wanted the oxygen mask to drop if the plane went down.

So George was all ready, packing a Cleveland Browns sweatshirt, a polar fleece sweater his son had given him years ago with the name Paine Webber on it (just the thing to wear to a country where every single bank had failed, taking the life savings of every Icelander with them), plus his brand new lightweight jacket with lapel stitching that reads "George Belden – Ohio State Fair Squash Champion", a desperately vain clinging to his glory days when he was on top of the food chain, so to speak.

Helena packed her winter coat and a pair of Cuddleduds, silky longjohns that made her look like an Amish housewife when she put them on under a skirt. Plus a tie-dyed hoodie, since she figured all Scandinavians are hippies.

Their one week in Iceland was always planned as almost two weeks, since the Beldens are retired and their lives have little of value to fill their dwindling time on earth. They decided to drive to Boston, stay overnight, fly to Reykjavik, live the Nordic life to the fullest, return, and mosey back to Ohio on no particular schedule.

It seemed like a good plan, giving them a chance to eat at many more restaurants while reassuring each other that they would be good children and only eat healthy things once they got home. This is a game they always play on vacation and always seem to forget the instant they cross the Ohio state line.

The plan was foolproof – until some jackass decided to schedule some joke of an event called the Boston Marathon, bringing 30,000 skinny people to Massachusetts on the very day the Beldens had something more important to do, like flying to Iceland. So they kicked the schedule back one day – now bringing in a conflict with the holiest day on the calendar: George's Monday Morning Golf Buddies League.

George decided that they could still keep the schedule even if he did golf in the morning, and besides, it might be the last time he would ever get to see the few people who willingly associate with him. So despite a weather report that called for a 95% chance of rain – as George says, pretty good odds, and it "never rains on a golf course" - he drove over to Fox Den in Stow, played nine miserable holes in a cold drizzle, but thanks to the masterful talents of teammate Bob Geiser, he managed to coax one American dollar out of the pocket of Mr. Timothy Reardon, enough money to finance exactly 11.6 miles of the trip as the Beldens headed out to Boston in that same chilly temperature they would – a foreshadowing – encounter 24 hours and half an ocean later. And that would turn out to be as warm as they would get for an entire week.

They left Kent about noon, and drove though rain hour after hour. But it didn't matter – they were on their way to Iceland, and every moment was an adventure as they scanned through station after station on the radio – they're seldom in the car long enough to justify Sirius – trying to find a station that didn't blare out Glenn Beck or Rush Limbaugh. An occasional snatch of a Herman's Hermits song was usually all they got until a station faded into the ether. And thus it continued through upstate New York until they reached Schenectady, the very name of which sounds like the punch line of an old Henny Youngman joke.

They had a wonderful room in the oh-so-elegant sounding Belvedere Hotel, and left the next morning only to hear on the radio of a bizarre connection to their past. Two years earlier, Bob Geiser and George had played golf at a wonderful, canyon-filled course called Capital Hills in Albany. Well, it turned out that one of those canyons had a landslide during the night because of the rain, the landslide blocked a creek, which then flooded a major roadway and forced them to detour around it.

Some people might call that an omen. Not the oblivious Beldens, though.

Helena had the foresight to negotiate a park-and-sleep in Saugus outside of Boston. They would park in the hotel lot for a week in exchange for staying there when they returned, plus they got a ride to Logan airport going and coming. Pretty sweet deal.

Except that Helena finally told George what she paid for it. Don't let her negotiate your next contract....They just hoped that there's a Kia with an Elizabeth Warren for President bumper sticker sitting there when they returned.

They had just enough time for a quick lunch before the pickup for Logan. Helena decided that Thai food would be a good prelude to an airplane flight for which they had not paid the bathroom tariff. Never let it be said that the Beldens have any ability to predict outcomes that would be obvious to a normal person. The facilities at Logan got a very demanding workout as they waited the five hours for the single daily flight of WOW airlines to Reykjavik at 6:55 PM Boston time.

The wait gave them plenty of time to watch all the Boston marathoners preparing for THEIR flights. They could tell who the runners were because they all wore huge medals around their necks, bowing them forward at the waist so it looked like a troop of Groucho Marx imitators gliding through the concourse. It turned out that several of them would be on the Beldens' flight, talking about how hot it had been in Boston. Race time temperatures had been in the 40's. Another omen missed by the Ohioans...

But the boarding was hassle-free – for the first 30 seconds. They had seats 9A and 9B, which Helena assured George were the seats by the emergency door, two seats in that row, with room enough to cross their legs and taunt everyone else packed into their 12 inch wide seats. Confidently, they strode back to those very seats, smiling at everyone they passed, stopped at the seats by the door, looked at the row number, and saw.....10A and 10B. They had been bamboozled by the on-line ticketing agent, and two little people, who had absolutely no use for that glorious legroom, brushed by them and plopped down.

Who whimpered more, George or Helena, is a moot point. A glance back revealed a 9C next to 9 A&B. Not only did they not get the big boy seats, some poor unsuspecting sucker would have to go flesh on flesh with the corpulent overflow occasioned by far too many late night Belden snacks.

"But," Helena whined to the attendant, "we paid for extra room."

"And indeed you have it," she said. "You get to recline your seat an extra 2 millimeters into the space in front of 10A and 10B."

But two events occurred simultaneously that made any further protests unnecessary. One, another passenger yelled out, "They're only one-third full – we each get our own row!"

And two – George wiped the tears from his eyes and looked up at the attendant. His gaze went up...and up...and continued up for a full three seconds, as he at last understood why this was going to be a great trip. He was once a volleyball coach, and would have given away one of his children (probably Garth, the youngest, although maybe he would have flipped a coin) to have had a player that looked like this.

Six foot three, blindingly blonde, stunningly gorgeous – but George, of course, cared only about the size of her hands and what a spiker she would have made under his tutelage.

Five hours of watching her glide slinkily in the aisle, thinking about how he would have coached her – the purest of thoughts, since his bride of 46 years was by his side, Helena having moved too slow to get a row of her own, the returning marathoners being much swifter afoot. At least both George and Helena got an extra six inches, splitting that extra seat in the row.

Reykjavik awaited, four hours ahead in time, one easy flight, landing in the middle of the night. Maybe even play golf that very first day, since the Weather Channel had promised a day in the 40's, the same as the Beldens had left behind.

Did I mention that weather forecasters are the world's biggest bullshitters? Well, that might be a story for another day...

Part 3

The WOW airbus landed at Keflavík International Airport at about 3 AM. By 4:00 AM they were at the Foss Lind Hotel.

It was daylight.

They had been in London many times, so they knew about extended daylight, but they were now in a place that was still light at 11 PM, and the sun began rising shortly after 3 AM. Clearly, they would need some heavy duty curtains to even approximate a good night's sleep.

The Foss Lind, bless its corporate heart, allowed them to go straight to their room, and even offered to let them eat breakfast beginning at 7, in essence allowing them to have an extra day's stay without charge. George and Helena were after only one thing, though – a couple of hours sleep, since their bodies were crying out that it was the middle of the night. Heading up to room 318, they opened the door to a very clean, not-as-small-as-expected room with two thin beds. Everything looked promising...

But the smell did not.

"Helena, this room smells like somebody just took a dump!"

"Well, if we complain, we won't have anywhere to crash. We'll ask for a different room after a nap." (Helena had been a fourth grade teacher and had spent 30 years in a classroom with pre-adolescent funk in the air.)

Resigned to sleeping in a malodorous miasma for at least a few hours, George grabbed a towel, turned on the hot water to wash away the residue of five hours cooped up with unwashed Boston marathoners on the plane – and instantly it became apparent where the dookie smell came from.

George's mother used to exile him every summer from the age of five on to his grandfather's farm, to give her two weeks' respite from his obnoxious behavior. On the farm, when he wasn't trying to steal his teenage uncle's Camel cigarettes, one of George's chores was to gather the eggs from the chicken coop every morning.

So George knew the smell of a rotten egg.

And the smell that came from the hot water tap was that smell.

Hours later, he would learn that, unlike in America, the water in the hot and cold pipes come from two completely different sources. The cold water was as delicious and odor free as anyone could ever ask for, some say the best on earth, but the hot water was pumped in straight from geothermal springs and carried the hellish remnants of sulfur, straight from the earth's core. If one had used the hot water, one ran the cold water for a minute to clear out the sulfur. And if one sat next to a person in a restaurant and they smelled of rotten eggs, well, that just meant that they were clean and neat and had just showered.

Despite the smell in the room, the two slept for six hours, and at 1 PM set off to face Reykjavik. They walked out of the hotel, and were please to see a huge map of the city on the corner.

And every single street name on that map was a jumble of letters not seen in English since the Dark Ages, formed neatly in words 40 or 50 letters long. In other words, these two Americans did not know where the fu** they were. So, in true Belden fashion, they began walking with absolutely no idea of a destination.

Fortunately, the Norse gods were smiling on them, because they were walking down Laugavegur, the main commercial street of Reykjavik, a street they would become very familiar with, since they would never stray from its worn cobbled path during their entire stay. It is a narrow one-way street where the sidewalk and road have identical bricking with no curb, so they never knew if there was a car just about to flip them over its hood. Thankfully, the Icelanders are the most polite drivers in the world, never seeming to be in a hurry, so it never became a problem – except when the wind blew one of Beldens into the middle of the road. But more on the wind – much more – some other day.

Wherever they go in the world, they book tours on Gray Lines. Gray Lines are like McDonalds; you know what you are going to get: pickup and drop-off at your hotel, a comfortable bus, a knowledgeable driver. And they knew the Gray Line office was on Laugavegur, so they kept walking until they found it. It was a goodly walk , with George whining about his feet, his knees, his hips, pretty much every part of his body every step of the way, but when they got there, they booked a tour for every day but one, starting that very day, with a trip to the world-famous Blue Lagoon. They were going to get naked.

But first they had to walk back to the hotel. And that's when the talking dogs appeared. And the dancing penguins. And the jogging traffic cones. And the six foot puffins. All traveling in packs of a dozen, doing conga lines in the middle of Laugavegur.

The guide books hadn't mentioned hallucinatory visions as a side benefit of Iceland.

Since everyone in Iceland speaks perfect English – besides Icelandic, every student learns English and one other language all the way through school – they asked a gentleman just what in the hell was going on.

"Oh, those are the high school graduates – they will be taking their final exams and they are celebrating. Each group of students decides on a different costume and they dance through the streets, making merry!"

Mind you – this is the day BEFORE they take their final exams.

At Maple Heights High School, where George had taught, they toilet papered the courtyard. At Windham High School, when Helena and George were seniors, Allan Kot put a dead skunk in the heating system. But dressing up as dogs and dancing in the street? How demented can you get?

But they had no time to watch these pseudo-canine antics any longer. They had to get their water shoes and swim suits before the Gray Line bus came.

The Blue Lagoon is just outside Reykjavik, and it can be smelled long before it can be seen. Water is taken from geothermal springs; some is sent through pipes to heat the houses and streets (in winter) of Reykjavik, some is used to spin turbines to generate electricity for the city and factories, and the run-off from the turbines is pumped into the Blue Lagoon, which has been turned into an economic goldmine.

Depending on how pampered you want to be, you can spend up to several hundred dollars at the Blue Lagoon. But the basic package just gets you entrance to this soupy blue pond, about four feet deep. After showering naked with a hundred other men (something George hadn't endured since he was a Windham Bomber football player), he put on his swim suit and sauntered outdoors about 25 yards to the pool.

It was 24 degrees outside. Those 25 yards were DAMN cold.

But once he entered the pool, he instantly knew why it was world famous. After adjusting to the reek of sulfur in the water, any ache or pain disappeared in the warmth. There are vats of white silica mud, also a byproduct of the industrial use of this water, which a person coats on any body part one wants to rejuvenate.

Despite his yearning to, George did not slather the white goop *under* his swimsuit. Some things cannot be restored to their former glory. Helena, however, loaded up her face with enough of this concoction to look like an actress trying out for a kabuki version of *On Golden Pond*, or maybe as a fill-in for Gene Simmons in a Kiss tour.

George and Helena spent over an hour drifting their way around the pool. Alcohol can be purchased lagoon-side, so many of the hundreds in the water with them were royally ripped.

After an hour, with limbs that had become like rubber in the heat, it was time to sprint those agonizing 25 yards back to the showers. After the return trip to the hotel, the weary Americans were too tired to go out in search of a restaurant, so they took their meal at the hotel eatery, where Helena ate lamb for the first time on the trip.

Did I ever mention that one of Helena's goals in life is to eat every single sheep on earth? No? Well, that's a story for maybe another time....

Part 4

Each morning found the Beldens in the basement of the Foss Lind, where the complimentary breakfast was a truly elegant repast. Everything one could want for carb loading for the day was laid out for the guests.

George usually had a peanut butter and jam sandwich, two tiny muffins with caramel in the middle, a piece of canary melon, and three espressos, since caffeine has no effect on him. Helena gorged on cheeses and several pieces of salami, never caring that she would be sharing close quarters with strangers on all day bus rides.

The second day of the Iceland adventure began with a tour of Reykjavik on a small Gray Line bus. As soon as the bus began the tour, George, who had not slept well that night before, immediately went into a deep coma, so if you, dear reader, are expecting a description of the capital of Iceland, go to your computer and google "Reykjavik wiki."

Instead, he will tell you why he didn't sleep. As soon as the windows were shuttered at 11 pm to block the still present daylight, the flaw in the Foss Lind became apparent: the walls were made of three thicknesses of onion-skin paper, and every sound in the neighbor's room, from persons no more than five feet from George's head, came though loud and clear.

The neighbors were French. French, and amorous. And taking their time.

Helena, of course, had begun her rhythmic snoring as soon as her head hit the pillow, and it was soon apparent that the neighbor's movements were synced to Helena's raspy cadence. It was too much for poor George to bear, an odious night to which you, poor reader, should not be subjected, so he will return to a more edifying description about what George remembers from the few moments he was awake on the Gray Line tour.

They saw the President of Iceland. They really did. They actually visited his house and parked at the front door. His name is Ólafur Ragnar Grímsson, he's been president since 1996, he has no security detail, and he has absolutely no powers whatsoever.

That's about all George remembers. You'll have to ask Helena if you want to know more. When they returned to the Gray Line office, they saw more talking dogs and puffins, as the graduation tests were one day in the future and the seniors were still out celebrating instead of studying. In fact, everybody was out celebrating, since this was a national holiday: The First Day of Summer.

Now, the calendar said that spring began only a month earlier, but Iceland only has two seasons: winter and summer, and summer begins whenever they say it begins. It may be 20 degrees and snowing, but damn it, it's summer. And on the first day of summer, everybody gathers in downtown Reykjavik and runs.

It's only a 5K race, so Icelanders of all shapes and ages run through the streets. Oh, there were a couple ringers who took it all seriously, but everybody else just seemed to be doing it because it was sunny and everyone who had been holed up for six months of perpetual darkness emerged, blinking, and said, hell, it's a good day for a race.

After the runners, walkers, strollers, and a few inebriated crawlers had cleared the street, George and Helena set off to find a museum unique in the world, the only one of its kind, which Helena's Silver Sneakers friend had urged her to visit, as his surrogate, and Helena had to whisper the theme of the museum as they hiked toward it.

"Say it louder, Helena. I thought I heard you say it was a dick museum."

She did not have to repeat it, because they had arrived.

It IS a dick museum. Created by a man named Johnsson, who had collected a penis from every Icelandic animal, including Homo Sapiens, and put them on display. Right down to a hamster dong you needed a magnifying glass to see. They even claim to have tallywhackers from Icelandic trolls and elves.

They didn't need to go in. They saw everything they needed to see from the window. And after the locker room at the Blue Lagoon the day before, George had seen enough junk to last the rest of his lifetime. It wasn't like the sperm whale penis was ever going to have any competition. They didn't even buy the tee shirt with the logo and motto: "This museum ain't for pussies."

Hiking through the incomprehensibly named streets of Reykjavik had given the Beldens a powerful hunger, so they stopped at a restaurant of Helena's choosing, "The Noodle Bar."

Here is the name again: "The Noodle Bar."

Who in their right mind considers noodles as a meal? The noodles in a huge bowl of spaghetti, maybe, but this bar, which had no alcohol on the menu, served noodles with broth. In George's world, that's called soup, and a soup-slurper he isn't.

Helena is. She sucked down a bowl of pasty wet ramen noodles, asked George if he was going to eat his, and swiftly tossed those down her gullet as well. And then she acted shocked when George marched to a bakery, ordered ham and brie with arugula on a baguette, and ate every single bite without offering her a taste.

She never asked to go to the Noodle Bar again.

It was time to roll back up Laugavegur to the hotel to wind down from the day. And that is when the battle for the computer began .

This was because Helena has no phone. The AT&T service she signed up for because the kid who lived next to them in Streetsboro works at the AT&T store, never mind that they were paying three times as much as anyone else for a monthly data plan that runs out if you even turn the phone on, let alone make a call - well, that plan would cost an extra $4 a minute if they made a call from Iceland, so she reluctantly turned it off.

She's was hurting. Bad. Like coming off heroin bad.

But the Hotel Lind – in fact, every establishment in Iceland – has free WiFi, so the computer was their link to the outside world, their source of information, since there are no English-language newspapers here. And Helena just HAD to find out what has gone on in the lives of her Facebook friends, who are mostly ex-students who barely remember her from fourth grade.

And George, of course, has thousands of bosom companions who cling to every word he posts on Facebook.

And here is the worst part. While in the pursuit of matrimonial equity they attempt to split their computer time equally, the one not on the computer has nothing to do. He or she might as well stick their thumb up their butt.

Oh, Helena could knit – she's already famous in Iceland for that, as you will find out in another chapter. Or she could read the books she stole from the Hotel Lind's library. But George doesn't knit, and he doesn't read the penny dreadfuls Helena favors. So – he could watch the TV in the room, right?

For all of its culture, for all of the things like health care, education, and classlessness in which it is ahead of the USA - Icelandic television sucks.

There are four channels. One is Icelandic C-Span, which involves one speaker jabbering for a while, then a quick pan to another person yelling "*Nein, nein*" and then everybody laughing.

One is a picture of a tree with snow on it. In seven days in Iceland the picture never changed. There is no sound.

One is an interview channel, on which the same female host interviews the same woman, who is apparently the fount of all knowledge, for 16 hours a day. It is the most interesting station because sometimes the camera operator dozes off and the camera angle drops to give the rare viewer a shot up the hostess's skirt.

Those three station are in Icelandic.

The fourth station is in English. It is the Cartoon Network. Apparently Icelandic children learn their pronunciation from Elmer Fudd, Daffy Duck, and Scooby Doo.

Part 5

The next day they got to sleep in, until 9 AM. The sun had already been up for six hours, but they had managed to get the curtains closed enough that their retinas had not been seared yet. They could have slept longer, but they had to get up because breakfast closed soon after, and it doesn't feel like they got their money's worth unless they are belching and farting as they head out for the day.

At breakfast, Helena discovered a different dish. It was gray and slimy and was obviously of fish origin, although it looked and smelled like something one discovers in the back of the fridge several years after purchase. Helena will eat anything she paid good money for, as long as the expiration date is within the current century. This is a girl who was raised on meals of sheep eye soup and cow udders, so she's game for anything.

Not this stuff. She poked and prodded it to make sure it was dead, and then hoisted a hunk to her lips. It's a good thing she was wearing the same thick gray top she'd would wear every day they'd be in Iceland – it's the only warm thing she brought – because she immediately spat out the viscous hunk.

"What was it?" George asked, glad it wasn't him that had been adventurous.

"I think it was herring, but I've never tasted it prepared that way. I think they cured it in that sulfur water, because it tasted like baby poo."

Never having had a hankering for finding baby poo at a smorgasbord, and appreciating the generations of diapers Helena had changed instead of him, George let it drop, silently reflecting that his friend Bob Geiser loves herring above all gourmet items, and wondering if the man had no taste buds at all.

George was also bold with his meal choice, choosing granola with milk instead of the Fruit Loops he generally seeks out at hotel breakfast spreads.

Their trip today was what is described as the Golden Circle, three stops in a circuit that covers the southeast corner of the 18th largest island on earth. The first stop was at the Thingvellir National Park, a large sunken area with a huge beautiful lake. Its claim to national fame is that Iceland's national assembly had been held there annually, from the first Viking settlement, for almost 1000 years, with loudmouths sitting on bales of hay and arguing about laws such as whether to eat their horses or not. The assembly was also a kind of Renaissance fair, so ale was sold and many laws were made by drunks. One man was in charge of remembering all the laws they made and reciting them annually, so he could pretty much change anything he wanted, which apparently happened when one of the reciters decided that they were all Christians now, which shocked the shit out of all the folks who were happy with Thor and Odin.

In 1798 they decided they could think better if they weren't freezing their asses off, so they finally made a building to meet in, and now Icelanders travel to Thingvellir and remember the good old days, like Americans travel to Salem Massachusetts and recall the fun times burning witches and such.

As they traveled to the next stop, Helena evinced a wide-eyed interest in the unvarying scenery. At a rest stop, previous travelers had gathered small stones and erected tiny monuments for no apparent reason. Helena decided to recreate items she had seen at the Phallic Museum the day before, to George's embarrassment.

The second leg of the Golden Circle was Geysir, which is exactly what it sounds like, the Icelandic version of Old Faithful. It's pretty impressive, and Icelandic authorities make absolutely no effort to keep people from standing right next to it, hoping to catch the 212 degree spray in their faces, scalding their visages, ghost-white from six months of complete darkness, and at least giving them some color. The Beldens watched from a distance and marveled.

The last stop was the Gullfoss Waterfall, the Icelandic version of Niagara Falls. It was the first of many waterfalls they would visit in the next few days. Spectacular, but memorable mostly for their efforts to avoid getting soaked as the tour guide urged them to walk down a steep path and stand right under it. Apparently this is a fun thing to do, as they would get the same advice at every waterfall from a string of different tour guides.

After their return, Helena decided it was time to sample another iconic Icelandic meal, the meat soup. They are immensely proud of it and one would think they would give it a more colorful name. Every restaurant serves it, and not a single one of them tells you WHAT meat is in this soup. Helena claims it's lamb, but George thinks back to that ancient assemblage at Thingvellir where they debated whether to eat their horses.

Helena ate two bowls, occasionally looking up, baring her canines and grinning wolfishly.

If Helena thinks it's lamb, there's no sense trying to disabuse her of the notion. After all, she's eaten every part of the animal, right down to lamb's knuckles one time in Wales, but that's a story for maybe another day...

Part 6

Today was the longest trip of their vacation. They got picked up by the Gray Lines at 7:30 AM, and returned to the Foss Lind at 10:30 PM. So the Beldens got to spend 15 hours with the only mean Icelander they met the entire week. This one could make people piss themselves with fear.

Her name was Helga, the tour director, and she was a direct descendant of Ilsa, She Wolf of the Nazi SS. Her favorite tactic was to say, "We will stop for five minutes, no more, no less." She trotted this out at rest stops, which she parceled out in proportion to how many times she heard a noise in the bus. Sometimes the passengers went hours holding it, whimpering in the firmly held belief that she had a cat-o-nine-tails tucked under her seat and wouldn't mind using it. When she allotted 15 minutes for a meal, nobody drank any liquid with it. One lady went the entire trip without ever leaving her seat. Helena suspected she was whizzing behind the bus when the rest of them were eating.

About three hours into the trip, George shifted in his seat, and the movement caught Helga's attention. Red rays coming out of her eyes like lasers on his forehead, she hovered over him and found his fatal flaw.

He didn't have his seat belt on. Since he wore five sweaters to withstand the cold and wind, that bulk, combined with his overall (but cute) chubbiness, prevented him from buckling the seat belt.

"You were told at the beginning of the trip that the law in Iceland demands that all seat belts be fastened at all times."

Now George knew why she wouldn't allow pee breaks: one has to unfasten the seat belt and break Icelandic law. But to make her retreat without hitting him, he pulled up all five sweaters and dug the cold metal into his alabaster gut, which left a dent that took two days to go away, a souvenir of the trip from Hell.

Their destination, 7 ½ hours into the trip, was the largest glacier in Europe. So in the interest of time, here is a description of the trip there. Lava, tundra, lava, tundra, lava, tundra. House. Lava, tundra, lava, tundra. Horse. Lava. Waterfall. Tundra. Glacier.

Notice that not a single human being was seen on the entire trip, outside of our bus. The country has 320,000 inhabitants, 319,900 of whom live in Reykjavik. The other hundred are trolls and elves.

Once the bus arrived at the glacial lagoon, they were supposed to go for a boat ride out among the icebergs that break off the Vatnajökull glacier. Icelanders really don't care that a boat ride among icebergs was why there was a movie called *Titanic*. But when the bus got there, the entire lagoon was literally clogged. George expected Helga to order everyone to help push the huge icebergs out of the way so the boat could be launched, but only one half-crazy Japanese tourist, whom they had nicknamed Smokey because he gave up all his rest stop and meal breaks to smoke two cigarettes at a time, was dumb enough to clamber out on the ice. Since the boat ride was canceled, Helga, rather than rebate what we had paid for the boat ride, said that we would get a free meal on the trip back.

Just as every condemned prisoner gets a last meal, George silently mourned.

Heels clicking on the floor of the bus, Helga strode the aisle with a pen and piece of paper. "Fiss, chizburger, or vaggieburger?" No one chose the vaggieburger, which was probably a vegetarian selection, but in a country that enshrines male sex organs in a museum, why take the chance?

Helga called the order to a roadside restaurant about an hour ahead, to give them time to prepare. When we were allowed off the bus and ordered to form a single line to get the food, the "fiss" was ready, but the burgers were not quite done, the unnamed animal which had donated its flesh having still been alive when Helga called.

Those getting "fiss" were given a plate, told to move down the line, and a sullen teenage girl plopped a ladle full of whitish, mucilaginous material onto the plate. Apparently in some alternate universe this was known as a fish stew, although Helena, who had chosen this, believed that they had just swished some fish bones through a vat of oatmeal to get this taste and consistency.

Suddenly, as if someone had turned a television to a 1979 rerun of *Saturday Night Live*, the cook behind the counter began bellowing "Chizburger, chizburger, chizburger" to alert the burger-choosers that their meal was ready. The Americans on the trip all began chuckling.

"Silence, or you will not eat."

Helga was not amused.

After eating in silence, with no desire to be beaten, the riders shuffled back to the bus, and not a sound was heard for the next five hours, since everyone wanted to get back to their hotel alive. This had to be the worst day a tourist had ever had – but one would be wrong to think that. And that's a story for another day...

Part 7

It was now Sunday, and the Beldens had nothing to do. No tours had been scheduled, stores did not open until noon, television was still a choice between Cartoon Network and the picture of the snowy tree that had not changed since their arrival. But after the previous day's trip with the Tour Guide from Hell, they needed the respite. So today the reader will learn why weather predictors are the world's biggest bullshitters, but it might take a while to get there.

The Beldens had been told that there was a famous flea market down near the harbor area which was open on Sunday. Going there would have entailed a walk of perhaps a mile from the Foss Lind Hotel. Despite George constantly whining that everything below his waist was completely non-functional (he meant hips, knees and feet, but Helena knew better), he figured that he could manage a mile on Laugavegur Street's brickwork, as long as Helena didn't act like she was marching toward a free lamb dinner and leave him far behind.

Just exactly WHY they wanted to go to the flea market was a mystery, as they had no money. Oh, they were not poor, as they had done their service to the youth of Maple Heights and Windham Ohio by teaching for 30 years, which entitled them to feed at the trough of the State Teachers Retirement System pension fund for as long as they were capable of staying alive. And since most of their restaurant meals at home consisted of Groupons and two-fer Quarter Pounders for filling out McDonald's surveys, they had shepherded their funds and were not living in squalor.

But they had been told – and it was true – that everything in Iceland could be paid for with a credit card. And Helena took that as an article of faith, confirming it by stopping at the Bonus grocery store and buying a log of Icelandic chocolate every time she passed it. Helena swore that Icelandic chocolate was far superior to the Cadbury chocolate she lives on when they visit England (she once jumped off a tour bus when she spotted the Cadbury factory, and it took several men to pry her from the locked gates).

But – and this is a big but – the Reykjavik flea market merchants do not accept credit cards. They want cold hard Króna. George had finally figured out that in Iceland one takes the listed price of something – for example, the oat cakes George has fallen in love with cost 500 Króna each – and then divide that number by 10, multiply that by 7, plug in a decimal point in the hundreds spot, getting a cost of $3.50 American (George was an English teacher and doesn't know jackshit about math but can intuit just enough to be dangerous). In the end it doesn't really matter what something costs, because he gives them a credit card and it doesn't cost him a thing because Helena pays all the credit card bills. Life's easy when one is a woman's love slave.

So, before he got distracted in that last paragraph, he was saying that cash was needed for the flea market – and the Beldens had no cash. Oh, George had gone to the Landisbank next to the Gray Lines office the first day and converted $50 into Króna, but he kept trying to give those stacks of funny colored paper to every service person he met, waiters, tour guides, desk clerks, for tips.

Helena seldom drops the F bomb, but she combined the participial form with nouns like "idiot", "dumbass", and other terms of endearment as she reminded George that YOU DO NOT TIP IN ICELAND! THE TIP IS ALREADY INCLUDED IN THE PRICE OF THE MEAL! Yes, she speaks in capital letters when it follows the F word and is directed at her husband.

So George had already given away most of their cash, and they wouldn't be able to buy anything at the flea market, so it was no real loss when they got no more than three blocks from their hotel when they had to stop – because all weather predictors are bullshitters.

It was the wind. The wind is the always-present specter that hovers over every activity. No matter how lovely the country, no matter how fascinating their cultural activities, it is always done in a 30 mile an hour wind. And the Icelandic powers-that-be have bribed the online Weather Channel to completely delete the column that says "wind chill."

A day might appear to be glorious – several had temperatures near 40 – but factor in the 30 mph wind and one is approaching a serious frostbite. The wind is constant and is capable of swinging 180 degrees within 10 steps. It is impossible to walk down the street without sticking out one's butt and rushing forward like a goat trying to ram someone who has invaded its pen.

That is, unless you are a native Icelander. In that case the wind does not affect you in the least. You can be talking to someone less than a foot away, and you can't hear a word they are saying, so you just keep saying "*Ja, Ja*" until they frown, and then you go "*Nein, Nein.*" They push their babies down the street in a stroller, and the baby will be wearing nothing more than a onesie. When they change a diaper, they just hold the baby's butt in the air and let the wind whisk it clean. These people are tough, tougher than two aging Americans, who spent an entire week dodging from doorway to doorway to avoid the gales of spring.

So the Beldens never made it to the flea market. In fact, it took them two hours to go three blocks, one doorway at a time. Their final shelter was a store that sold ice cream, which Icelanders eat 365 days a year.

Hell, when in Iceland, do as the Vikings do...and Magnum ice cream bars are SO good...and tomorrow was another day – and another story.

Part 8

She's known in Iceland as the knitting woman. In the USA, Helena is acclaimed far and wide as one of the most diligent quilters alive. She will make a quilt for anyone on any occasion. Did you have a bowel movement you were particularly proud of? Helena will make a quilt to celebrate it. Did you just have a baby? There's a baby quilt coming, although she may not finish it until your baby has completed his first tour of duty with the Army. But in Iceland, she's known as the knitting woman, because she does have many more talents than quilting.

Whenever she goes on a trip, she takes her knitting. I don't want to insult any other knitters out there, but it's pretty much a mindless activity. It takes no brain power, and only requires an occasional "damn it" when one drops a stitch or tangles the yarn so badly it takes an hour to unravel. So it was a perfect activity for the cross-country jaunts by bus that occupied the majority of the Beldens' time in Iceland.

The object she was knitting was long, rectangular, and purple and white. It could have been anything, but would have been most useful if she had completed it and wrapped it around her head to block the painful Icelandic wind. But no, she claimed it was a receiving blanket for a pregnant stranger she had met in a grocery store check-out line, so the clack-clack of her needles was an omnipresent background to the droning of tour guides trying to say something original about the moss that covers 99% of Iceland's land surface. She also used the needles to jab George if his snoring was bothering the other passengers.

For their final day in Iceland, and having gone on every trip the Gray Line offered, they decided to go on a nebulously-described tour with another line, Sterna, which did not own any big buses and ran only stick-shift mini-vans. The tour was scheduled to visit the Blue Lagoon, not to bathe in it but only to smell the sulfur stink, and then ramble aimlessly around the southern peninsula of Iceland for six hours. Since most of their retirement life fits the description of "aimless," it sounded pretty good to them.

Their driver, Mik, picked them up. A bearded fellow in a wool sweater not many months removed from a now-naked sheep, he gunned the van through the streets of Reykjavik while informing them in a thick accent that they would be alone today, so they were going to get the ride of a lifetime. As he seemed more jovial than the dominatrix who had been their tour guide the trip before, they were ready for it. Helena would do no knitting today.

Mik started out the road trip by talking about Icelandic rock music. Now, George knew that there was an Icelandic Rock and Roll Hall of Fame, located in a broom closet somewhere in Reykjavik, which celebrated the achievements of Sigur Rós, whose music can induce sleep almost instantly, and Björk, the elfin singer more famous for wearing swans around her neck than her singing. But Mik wanted to talk about Of Monsters and Men, the latest Icelandic craze. George had never heard of them, and was ashamed to admit that when he googled them that night, they have the number four song on the Billboard Adult Alternative Chart, "Crystals." George also saw why Mik was so interested in them – he looked exactly like their lead singer, who also bore more than a passing resemblance to George's son, Garth.

After speeding the van past the Blue Lagoon, Mik instead chose to take the Beldens to the source of the waters of the lagoon. They spent the next hour visiting numerous mud flats from whence bubbled both hot steam and the most ghastly flatulent smell to which the earth could give rise. And Mik was not content to just have them view these; he directed them to the spots where the wind would best coat them with this fetid stench. Since they had planned to wear these same clothes on the airplane tomorrow, he was guaranteeing that they would be the least-liked ugly Americans in ages.

George had earlier mentioned that he had been hoping to play golf in Iceland when they were planning the trip. But as it turned out, even if he had been willing to play in a wind in which he would have to putt with the driver lest the ball come spinning back to him, none of the courses had yet opened for the season. But Mik decided to grant George his wish, so the next stop was one of Iceland's many golf courses. George got to stand on the first tee and have his photo taken with the course as a backdrop. The wind immediately billowed his clothes, so that his already tubby physique now resembled the Stay Puft Marshmallow Man from *Ghostbusters*. At the very moment when Helena snapped his picture, the wind actually blew the watch off his arm.

By now it was time for lunch, and Mik drove to a seaside village, Grindavik, famous for its fishing, and also the corporate headquarters of several fish companies. Mik, a socialist, stopped in front of each one to denounce the f***ing capitalist swine who had gutted Iceland's economy. The Beldens, old-time lefties themselves, enjoyed his rants immensely. They then stopped at Bryggjan, a tiny restaurant in the corner of a shop that sold rope to mariners, and were treated to a peppery lobster stew and the stories of the old-timers sitting inside, none of which they understood, but they knew by cadence when to laugh. The last thing they were shown were the wood carvings of a local artist who had made small busts of heroes of Iceland. One of them was Mick Jagger.

Continuing on, Mik decided to go completely off-road to travel to a very famous spot known to bird watchers around the globe. George, who has rods and screws in his back, grimaced at every bounce over hidden chunks of lava as the gears of the transmission groaned and screamed in protest. Halfway to the destination, an unbridged river blocked the route, and Mik thought for quite a while before deciding he was driving a van rather than a boat. He then backed up the entire way from which he had come, hitting every lava block in reverse. They felt the same no matter what direction he hit them from.

Traveling then on a nicely paved road that led to the exact same spot, the Beldens were stunned to see that the destination of the hegira of many a bird watcher was a statue of a bird that had not existed on the earth since 1844 – the great auk. Early Icelanders decided that auk omelets were the cat's pajamas, and every time an auk laid an egg, it ended up scrambled in some Nordic breakfast dish.

They never figured out that no eggs means no new auks. But they made a statue of the bird gazing forlornly at its former nesting ground on a cliff. That cliff is also the windiest spot in Iceland, which nearly resulted in Helena pitching off the edge as a sacrifice to a species made extinct by human stupidity.

It was now mid-afternoon, with only time for two more stops. The first one was a fascinating site one can only find in Iceland – the point at which the Europe and American tectonic plates are grinding against each other, the very reason why there are volcanoes in Iceland but also earthquakes in Europe and the United States. It just looks like a big ditch, and since they didn't have a thousand years to watch it move an inch or two, they settled for a picture of Helena astride two continents, the one of her birth and the one where she has brought George his greatest joy (Helena suggested that last line).

The final stop of the trip was Viking World, a museum which contains actual artifacts from the settlement of Iceland in the 9th century, as well as from the voyage of Eric the Red, described by Mik as a "troublesome man who was banished from Iceland for some killings," to Greenland, and the travels of his son, Leif the Lucky, so called because he managed to avoid being murdered in a snit by his father, to Vinland, thus being the first white claimant to discovering the continent the Native Americans had occupied for millennia.

But two other exhibits dominated the museum. Oddly, one was a picture of former President Bill Clinton eating a hot dog – Iceland is bonkers over hot dogs, which, like meat soup, contain flesh from any hapless creature which had wandered near the abattoir– with a caption mocking Clinton for having the hot dog with only mustard, instead of loading on all the Icelandic condiments, including twigs, bark, and remoulade, a sauce made with mayo, capers, mustard, and herbs.

The other exhibit was a Viking vessel - well, a recreation – that had actually been sailed across the ocean to New York City in the year 2000 to celebrate Leif the Lucky having escaped the patriarchal ax of Eric the Red. In the bow of the ship are two ghostly figures arguing about whether to visit the Empire State Building or an Atlantic City casino when they got there.

And with that, the adventures of the Beldens in Iceland ended. Mik drove them back to the Foss Lind. As he was by far the most entertaining tour guide they had in Iceland, George forked over the last of his Króna as a tip, ignoring Helena's protests that there was still chocolate to be purchased, and they collapsed onto their tiny beds to slumber until it was time to go to the Keflavík International Airport for the return trip on WOW airlines to the States.

The airport was comfortable but featureless, the boarding was on time, the plane was 2/3 full so no one was cramped, and the only thing of note is that that the half male, half female crew of airline attendants was comprised of exact clones of the four members of ABBA. A smooth flight, a flawless touch down, and the Beldens were headed home, have pillaged another country on their road to world conquest, leaving future American tourists to clean up their mess.

The Beldens Go To Bermuda 2016

This is going to end badly, George thought. Belden vacations always do. The only real question is how terribly it was going to begin.

Everybody has a bucket list. Helena's starts in the Cadbury factory in Bournville, England, where she'll watch workers stirring the hazelnuts into the chocolate. That's it. It's a damn short list. She never plans to leave the factory once she's there. They'll have to come in with a forklift to get her corpse out.

George, on the other hand, has an extensive bucket list, which cannot be put in print because most of the items have the word "coed" in them, preceded by verbs that are physically impossible for someone of his age and girth.

One of the few things that can be reported without censorship, though, is an inexplicable desire to go to Bermuda. The place where shorts were invented, where he can display his alabaster gams without shame, whitewashed legs that reflect enough solar energy during Ohio summers to power small towns. Bermuda, sitting enticingly at the same latitude as North Carolina, but far enough in the gulf stream to warmly waft away the shivering memories of their frosty voyage to Iceland.

Besides, this year is the 50th anniversary of Helena being desperate enough for a prom date to say yes to George's impassioned importuning, after he overcame his morbid fear of large dogs to walk by her German shepherd (later discovered to be too lazy to bark, let alone bite) to ask for a date, so he figured he owed her something, though cheaper than a big diamond, which can't be eaten, after all.

Which is why George is sitting in the middle of the ocean on a cruise ship with 2000 other passengers after having sworn that he would never ever take another cruise after Helena and her Windham Ohio teacher cohorts allowed one of their less-than-worldly colleagues to book a Caribbean cruise through the Pied Piper Travel Agency. Go ahead and google it. It specializes in LGBTQ trips. The best part about that cruise was that George never got to hear as much ABBA as he did over those seven days. The fancy and frolic of their fellow passengers furnished a lifetime of unanticipated memories for those naïve Windhamites, as you will read in a later chapter.

The Beldens have been on so many trips that preparation is automatic. Helena is the tour director, since she enjoys nothing more than sitting at a computer eighteen hours a days for months, swearing because a website isn't working right or the hotel we want is already booked, all the while watching CNN and dropping F bombs every time someone badmouths her hero Hillary. In the end everything works out. Helena packs the week prior to departure; George begins about 10 minutes before leaving the driveway. How much time does it take to load two pairs of underpants that can double as beach tents, after all?

Because George has a fear of cooties, he always carries a bottle of Purell in his coat pocket, a coat he gently placed in the car in anticipation of needing it when standing in line waiting to board the ship.

Helena, eager to get out of Kent, tossed her suitcase squarely on top of George's coat, smashing the bottle of Purell, guaranteeing both that the car would reek of alcohol if they got stopped by a cop during the drive, and that George would probably catch Norovirus before they even got to their stateroom. Fortunately, neither of those things happened, and the boarding process, after a night spent in Baltimore, with a shuttle from the hotel to the dock, was fairly uneventful.

In fact, because the Beldens are Gold Club members, having accumulated enough points to qualify for the 10% discount on tanzanite jewelry "found in one now-flooded cave in South Africa but available to you only on board this very ship," and "rare art" sold on every single cruise ship, they were also granted the perk of not having to wend their way though the line of first-time travelers chattering happily about all the things they heard about cruises, including the unlimited crustaceans at Lobster Night in the dining hall. Oh, if they only knew the disappointing mudbugs they will find on their plates that evening; larger things have crawled out of the polluted Cuyahoga River in downtown Kent Ohio.

The Beldens came on board the *Grandeur of the Seas* at 10 AM. You might have heard of the ship. Besides being one of the smallest cruise ships still afloat, it is the same ship that caught fire several years ago near the Bahamas, necessitating every passenger to be flown home. Of course, Royal Caribbean Lines has done its damnedest to keep THAT fact well hidden.

Knowing that the staterooms would not be available for several hours, they commandeered two chairs in the central atrium to watch the parade of humanity that always swirls around during that anticipatory stage. One of the best parts is the cat-and-mouse game played by people trying to smuggle booze onto the ship to avoid paying for the pleasure of getting drunk enough to vomit in the pool. They always get caught. The funniest ones are the old men who think the bulge in their pants will pass as just another boner, when everyone who looks at them knows the last drop of testosterone fled their gonads eons ago.

The downside of people watching is having to deal with the corporate barkers trying to shill the indecently overpriced "extras" that the cruise line uses to pad their profits. No, I do not want to pay $13 dollars a day for all the Coke I can drink. I take three different diuretics a day just to keep my arteries from exploding – why would I want to spend the whole day in my cabin peeing even more? How about signing up for the all-you-can-eat lobster brunch on the third day? $85? Such a deal...lemme think about that...

Suddenly came the announcement that everyone was waiting for – the cafeteria was open for lunch. Despite having eaten a free hotel breakfast only two hours earlier, the Belden credo of "let's eat again real soon," said at the conclusion of every meal, kicked in, and George and Helena headed for the lunch line along with a stampede of people determined to inhale everything in sight just to get their money's worth. George stopped in a restroom along the way, where a sign requesting guests to wash their hands was placed rather bizarrely as an aiming point inside the urinal, as if beckoning the tinkler to both relieve himself and then lave in the spray that followed.

George commenced trotting around the serving lines to reconnoiter before focusing on the most caloric offerings, when he heard a obscenely hideous cackle behind him, a wet sickly suctioning noise, and a set of teeth clattered to a stop against his left foot....but that's a story to be told another day.

Part 2

If you have never been on a cruise, you have never enjoyed the thrill of a stateroom. If, however, you have ever experienced a premature burial, you have some idea of what it is like. Every inch of space is dual functioned. The toilet doubles as the writing desk – in fact, Helena has just asked George to quit typing for a minute, as she has some official, malodorous business to attend to. The bed, however, has no discernible function at all, as it is absolutely impossible for anyone to use it for its intended function. Royal Caribbean cobbled together some left-over plywood from the construction phase, to which they glued some old tablecloths. The pillows are the rolls of toilet paper to be used later in the cruise. Needless to say, George, whose bulk is much more sensitive than the Princess and her legendary pea, did not anticipate any shuteye anytime soon.

A requirement on every cruise is the "muster drill," where everyone gathers on deck to be informed about the dignified way to die if the ship goes down. Three things are inevitable. One, the crew will try to shoehorn the entire population of the ship into the smallest possible space, leading to two, everybody complaining as loudly as possible about how they can't breathe and the old guy behind them is rubbing their butt, which causes number three, nobody can hear a word about what they are there for. All in all, it's pretty useless, but today's muster drill had the added benefit of a kid yelling that he didn't like mustard and nobody could make him eat mustard. That child will be the last one in the lifeboat, if and when.

As he predicted, George did not sleep one jot the first night on the ship, while Helena rasped her way through her usual comatose night. As the rosy fingers of dawn arrived (as Homer (the Greek, not Simpson) once said), it became apparent that the boat was trapped in the middle of a very turbulent ocean. Bering Sea, "Deadliest Catch," 40 foot swells with whitecaps as snowy as Bernie Sanders' hair, turbulent.

The Beldens have cruised in harsh waters before, but George had never been so dedicated to his stationary bike routine. At home, he goes every single day to the Kent State Wellness Center to ride the bicycles in his shorts. He knows that there are many many young female students for whom that is the high point of their day.

So George did what he planned to do every morning: he went to the Vitality Fitness Center, strode past the aged crones waiting to pay Scandinavian masseuses to rub their parchment-like torsos, and hopped on the nearest bike.

He pedaled. The ship rode the waves, and he doggedly pushed on, determined to get in his forty minutes and burn off 240 calories, the better to justify the double crème brulee he intended to consume at dinner. He realized that the handlebars were loose, but that just added one more rocking motion to the workout. And then he looked out the windows at the sea.

He suddenly realized that if he sat on that machine one more second, he was going to puke, voluminously. All of the orange juice, eggs, oatmeal, waffles, blood sausages, mangoes, and innumerable other foodstuffs which he had gobbled for breakfast were going to be upchucked in one gloriously panoramic rainbow of gore. For the first time in his life, George was seasick.

George's younger brother David was the person for whom Dramamine was invented. David has had motion sickness his entire life, or so he claims. On family vacations, David ALWAYS got a window seat, so that he could hang his nose out of a cracked window, huffing the fresh air like a pathetic beagle. In fact, his moaning was decidedly hound-like, but the sibs always figured that he had just found the perfect scam to always get to ride shotgun. And Mom, who didn't especially like any of her six offspring, always had a soft spot in her heart for that prissy little faker, so George the family bully was never able to extract his pound of flesh for this ingenious technique David had stumbled upon.

But now, a half-century later, George discovered empathy. It would be a battle between the urge to purge and the long-respected Belden dictum that "if it goes down my throat, it ain't ever coming out that end again."

Heading back to the stateroom, he threw himself on the rock shelf that passed for the bed, calling Helena's name in vain for hours (it seemed) until she finally returned from flirting in the hot tub with aging men who used the roiling bubbles of the water to disguise the farts that they no longer had the muscle tone to contain within their sphincters. Begging her to go the the "Royal Shoppe" to get some Dramamine, Helena was torn between the desire to watch George suffer, always a cheap source of entertainment, or to get him some medicine that might stem the uncomfortable prospect of sleeping in regurgitated slime that evening. Pragmatism and self-preservation won, and she fetched a box of sea-sickness pills priced as if they were semi-precious gems. Royal Caribbean knows how to plunder those in the greatest need at a cost of whatever the market will bear.

If a product called Bonine ever needs an endorsement, George is willing. One hour after George uttered the previously-never-heard words "you go to dinner without me," he made his entrance at the Great Gatsby Dining Hall smiling and ready to get to work.

Earlier in the day, George and Helena had both fretted about what to wear on "formal night," when the cruise line recommends tuxedos and cocktail dresses. Helena had decided on the shift she used to cover her bathing suit, assuming it had dried after her hot tub encounters, and George had nixed the New Balance shoes he wore when he mows the lawn for the deck shoes with a hole cut in the side to accommodate the enormous, angry bunion that appears at the least opportune moments.

They were far from the worst dressed.

The Beldens were served their meals by Juliana, a pleasant young lady whose nameplate said she was from Brazil. Drawing on their limited fund of knowledge about that country, Helena asked her if she was going to be in the upcoming Olympics. George asked her if it hurt too bad when she got a Brazilian wax. No one will ever accuse them of being uninformed travelers.

After dinner, they headed to the theater to be entertained by a smarmy acapella group called Edge Effect, whose website is notaboyband.com. Since they averaged about 40 years old, the website name was superfluous AND overkill. The lead singer fancied himself a Justin Timberlake clone, if Justin wore shoes three sizes too small and grimaced every time he had to put his feet down. It was one of the worst performances the Beldens had ever endured on a cruise ship, and they had actually, several years ago, seen one singer try to to portray the Trapp Family from *The Sound of Music* AND the children from *The King and I* in a Broadway medley.

Having spent the day fighting nausea, both ocean-induced and from watching the sad theatrical offerings, George decided to spend another night trying to find a single comfortable sleeping position while listening to Helena honk away like a toy saxophone in the lips of a demented child. The rhythmic thumping from the next room did, for a moment, capture his intellectual curiosity, but that's a story best left for another day.

Part 3

Bermuda, you ask. What about Bermuda itself? Please, the dear reader begs, describe the tanned, lightly sweating bodies barely covered with tiny fabric strips in strategic places, cavorting on the pink sand beaches, beckoning the Beldens to abandon all sense of morality and gambol with them, as nymphs and satyrs are wont to do.

Well, since the entire purpose of the enormous amount of money the Beldens had squandered on this caprice was to spend time in this alluring island nation, Helena had chosen a cruise that allotted 25 hours in Bermuda.

Think about that for a second. 25 hours. Between docking, eating many enormous meals on the ship, and fighting Morpheus for yet another night, that left exactly eight hours to experience the majesty of this regal British colony, before the ship reversed course and took us back to Baltimore, the city which had stolen the REAL Cleveland Browns and still had a Modellian stench about it.

So Helena, the tour director, decided that the Beldens would do two shore trips, neither of which involved a single glimpse of a lithe nude body, much to George's fantasy-bursting chagrin. The first, on the day of arrival, would be a ferry ride from the Royal Navy Dockyard, where the ship was based, to St George's, which was founded well over two centuries ago and thus could not have been named in honor of Helena's current husband who was, after all, Henry VIII in a previous lifetime (Helena believes she was Anne Boleyn, and has been extracting retribution for a misunderstanding about a beheading ever since. Leave it to a woman to never forgive and forget...). The second trip the next day would be a round trip bus tour of the entire island, which better serve champagne on board, since it cost $99 each.

The first day ferry ride to St George's was completely uneventful. The transportation system of Bermuda is incredibly well organized. Since visitors are banned from driving a car in this tiny country with only three main roads, the ferry and bus lines are tightly coordinated and run precisely on time. The ferry both left and arrived within one minute of schedule. In other words, miss the return ferry, and you were 21 miles from the ship.

Let that sink in for a minute – because the Beldens didn't.

St George's is beautiful, a United Nations heritage city. There is not a scrap of trash on the street (they later learned the government burns all trash the country generates for energy). No dogs ran the alleys, fouling it by crapping everywhere, as on the overrated Mediterranean island of Santorini. As a matter of fact, there was not even a living creature to be seen. It was Stephen King-ishly, Walking Dead-like, Bermuda Triangly quiet. Granted, it was a mid-week afternoon, but where the hell was everyone?

Not inclined to think too deeply, the Beldens decided to get their drink on.

They headed for a watering hole that at least had its door open and ordered two pints of Strongbow Cider from the bartender, a toothy older gent who scoffed when asked if he knew about any sports other than the cricket matches showing on every television in the place.

Who won the Kentucky Derby? He knew about Nyquist. Did the Cleveland Cavaliers win their series against the Hawks? "Who the hell cares?" he said. "I'm a Celtics fan."

Rather than see George break the man's arm the way Kelly Olynyk had broken Kevin Love's the previous year, Helena diverted the publican's attention by asking if they had WiFi, and did it require a password? "It is free," she learned. "But does it need a password?" "It is free. It is free." By this time she was grinding her teeth, pissed off that he wouldn't answer her question, when he reached over, grabbed her phone, and tapped "itisfree" in the password box. Abbott and Costello would have been proud.

Several drinks on the outdoor patio later, Helena was feeling romantic and asked the waitress to take a picture of her with her handsome hubby. After the girl, whose vision was better than the love-struck sexagenarian, finished her laughing spasm, she snapped a picture of the two alcohol-addled tourists. If one examines the resulting portrait closely, one can see two things: neither of them is wearing a watch, and, in the distance, the ferry departing for the Royal Dockyards.

Uh-oh.

Shocked from her Bacchus-induced haze, Helena remembered that the bus lines, if ridden long enough, would eventually reach the dockyards, so, after dodging several cars because they had forgotten that these British colonials drive on the wrong side of the road, they found themselves on a near-empty bus bound for the capital city of Hamilton, where they could transfer on a bus to the other end of the island. It was at this point that they discovered that the municipal buses are also the school buses of the nation. And the school day had just ended.

At every stop, more and more primary students poured into the creaking vehicle. They were all in uniforms, and were extremely polite, but they were, after all, rugrats, an age group Helena had fled upon her retirement years earlier. One particularly vociferous ten year old told everyone on the bus that he couldn't wait to get tattoos, but his mother told him he had to wait until he was fifteen. He already had a list of tattoos he was going to get and in what order. Most were Bermudian sports heroes, conveniently portrayed on a wall he pointed out in Hamilton, although he might be taxed to explain a Justin Bieber tattoo to his grandchildren.

The ride to Hamilton was interminable, and the second leg was no less so. The bus stopped at every single pull-off on the road, so a 10 mile trip took almost two hours. As the Beldens, the very last passengers, exited the bus, Helena decided she need one more nip before boarding the ship. Stopping into the bizarrely named "Frog and Onion" pub, she ordered two ciders, for which she paid $21, helping her decide that all of her imbibing would be done on board the ship from then on.

Refusing to acknowledge that they were much too stupid to be allowed to roam about unsupervised, the witless Ohioans left the following morning to join the tour of the entire island. The bus driver, Calvin, was a walking encyclopedia who knew everyone on the island, and so was able to tell the riders exactly who lived in every house the bus passed. In fact, since Calvin was cursed with a bit of a stutter, he said everything twice, which really did give the passengers more than their money's worth. But a five hour bus trip without chattering children was a blessing, so by the end of the trip, both Beldens agreed that indeed Bermuda is the cleanest, most beautiful island nation in the western hemisphere, one to which they will return sooner rather than later.

The last leg of the trip was to be another ferry ride, no more than 10 minutes, from Hamilton to the ship. It was now 1:20, the gangway would rise at 2 PM for departure – no problem. Except the transfers that Calvin handed them for the ferry were one week out of date....but that's a story best told some other time.

Part 4

Mirrors...have I mentioned the mirrors? They're everywhere. Not counting the bathroom, there are FIVE full-length mirrors lining every wall in this tiny stateroom. As if gazing at our porcine physiques, which are growing geometrically with every visit to the all-you-can-eat dining rooms, is going to make us want to put on bathing suits and march around a pool where there are over a thousand pairs of eyes either following our every move or rolling back in their sockets in abject horror. Who decided that mirrors are the proper décor on cruise ships?

So, on the 36 hour trip back to Baltimore, the Beldens are spending as little time in the stateroom as they possibly can, which means that they find a nook in which to read, or they participate in the contests that are held hourly for the chance to win some cheapass trinket with the cruise line's name emblazoned on it. George has, on occasion, entered musical trivia contests despite being banned from them on one cruise for pointing out that several songs in a "British 60's" contest ("I Got You Babe"?) were in fact not from the United Kingdom at all. The staffer running that contest at first blamed "the corporate suits who make up these contests" and later told George to be very careful about knocks on the door that night. George blames his mouthiness on that old demon rum.

Helena, on the other hand, is a avid participant. She proudly pranced up to a quietly-reading George and announced that she had just won the History trivia contest, getting 12 out of 20 mind-bogglers such as "Which Lenin was in the Beatles, John or Vladimir?" She won a yellow highlighter for that triumph. None of the other contests were of mutual interest, but Helena did agree to go with George to the "Name That Big Band Tune" contest. Since most of the contestants had been around when Edison introduced the first gramophone, George did not expect to win, which he didn't, since his main experience with big band records was stomping to bits, at the age of three, all the shellac 78's his father and mother had treasured since their teens, because he was afraid of Nipper, the dog logo on every RCA disc. However, he had to pretend he didn't even know her when Helena believed that she recognized one of the songs and began to sing "Baa Baa Black Sheep" to the tune of "Bye Bye Blackbird". Since the poor girl begins to salivate whenever she sees a sheep in a field, her mutton-headed mistake had to be forgiven.

On the way back to their room, the Beldens passed once more though the central atrium, where a chameleon-like Guatemalan band was playing romantic ballads. Twice a day they changed their clothes and hiked out by the pool, where they transformed into a reggae band, thumping out Mayan versions of Rastafarian hits by Bob Marley.

At this particular moment, though, there was an evil confluence, as George had just found out about the ill-fated voyage of this very vessel, the *"Grandeur of the Seas"*, in 2013, when the ship burned and the entire passenger list, as many souls as live in the Belden's natal village of Windham, Ohio, had to be airlifted off. As that information turned over in his mind, the female lead singer started belting out the "Love Theme from 'Titanic'" in a voice resembling Celine Dion's only in gender. It was perhaps history's worst choice for a song on a cruise ship, let alone THIS cruise ship.

The one place on the ship the Beldens avoided was the casino, although Helena, when she gets rooted to a penny slot she likes, can tear through the best part of a five dollar bill in record time. George has a profound dislike of watching pensioners hooked up to oxygen tanks feverishly hoping for one last big score before crapping out of this world. Besides, this cruise was precipitated by the 50th anniversary of their first date, and Helena had gambled and lost on that one, so why chance an even worse losing streak?

Because Royal Caribbean allows self-deportation in the morning (and Mitt Romney thought he invented that term), the Beldens would be leaving the ship at 7:45, so they agreed that a 6:00 AM alarm would leave them plenty of time to pound down a few thousand more calories before departure. However, one of the Beldens, the one in charge of the alarm, forgot that Bermuda is one hour ahead of Baltimore in time zones, and her phone was still set for Bermuda time, so at 5 AM, the Beldens were the first people to arise on the third level. It would be a long tired drive home, and it would take a lot of coffee. After the fourth cup, George tossed down his daily collection of 20 or so pills that keep him alive – and then realized that all of the diuretic (aka "pee") pills he had skipped over the vacation had been accumulated in that pile he had just swallowed – but that's a story of a ballooning bladder and a six hour drive in which I'm sure no one is interested.

Interlude – George Has Surgery 2013

Only a few of my friends and family have known that for the last six months I have slowly been losing the ability to walk, or even stand for more than a few moments. I had devised work-arounds to hide it, and even to be able to continue golfing (as long as a certain golf partner didn't take forever to putt). But rather than face life in a wheelchair, The Beldens decided that, even at my advanced age, they had to deal with it. So last Wednesday I had spinal surgery. The operation was much more extensive than the surgeon expected (an overnight in the hospital lasted four days, and I now have several pounds of hardware in my back).

Post-surgical observation #1:

In the primal swamp of pain that was my sole awareness for the first five days, two goals gave me the will to endure: the dream of being able to shower for the first time- to scrub away the enormous amount of crud that adheres to someone covered with numerous spots where tape had been placed, and the equally glorious thought of my first triumph over the medically-induced constipation that comes with spinal surgery. I didn't care which came first; I desired each one like I had put it on my Santa wish list.

On day 6, I was released to shower. Helena had winched me onto the shower stool, I sat there with an umbrella held up so I wouldn't get heart-failure from the water as it warmed up. And then – dream number two decided to come true. AT THE PRECISE SAME MOMENT. It would be too much information to tell you which choice I made, because there really was NO choice.

God bless you, Saint Helena. There is a special place in Heaven for you. And I will cherish and honor the expression on your face until the end of my days on earth.

Post-surgical observation #2:

I am nicotine free for the first time in 50 years.

It's amazing what an insurance company can accomplish by denying payment for a surgery that could run half a million dollars, if you have nicotine in your system. That's a sphincter-clincher.

I quit smoking 25 years ago but immediately became the prototypical ex-coach dipper and chewer. Then 10 years ago I wanted to quit dipping, so I tried gum. Got addicted to that. There's nothing more humbling than sitting for hours looking on eBay for gum approaching its expiration date on which I could underbid some other junkie to feed my Nicorette jones.

It took the patch, and a death panel at an insurance company, to do the trick. Holy crap, was getting off nicotine hard after half a century, but I did it.

But if YOU have a bad back and are facing surgery, let this be a warning. There's a $$hitLoad of other things you can do with half a million bucks.

Post-surgical observation #3:

I have used Breathe Right nasal strips since the day they were invented. My sinuses close up at night and I can't breathe through my nose. I also occasionally wore them in class if I had a head cold, oxygen being preferable to comments about my goofy looks. But one of my caregivers found a new use for them: as a deadly weapon.

A Breathe Right is centered over the nose and then smoothed down, so that it remains springy, tugging from the nose flare upward. But the unnamed caregiver (married almost half a century...) decided it would work better if it was folded into a V, tugging upward from near the center of the nose. So she decided to do just that. She centered the device on my nose, and then proceeded to pinch it into the V shape by using her thumb and index finger to completely cut off my already-narrow nasal passages. Being unable to breathe, I began to flop around like a beached monkfish, from which she deduced it was not such a good idea to be charged with murder by Breathe Right and have the case bandied about by Nancy Grace and her sordid ilk, so she released her death-pinch and I was able to quit thrashing about.

On the one hand, I was able to forget my back pain for a moment as I struggled to live. On the other hand, I have been using Breathe Right for 25 years and they always peel off easily in the morning. This one was applied with so much force that it took off all the skin on the right side on my nose, so I now bear an unsettling resemblance to Skeletor.

Beldens are used to our name being misspelled. Beldon (the way it sounds) and Belding (courtesy of the old tv show *Saved By the Bell*) are the usual. Occasionally there is the one that unintentionally satirized my infamous size: Mr. Building. After all, we Beldens all thought our name was meaningless until my genealogist brother Deane Belden uncovered our origins in the town of Baildon, England, from which we were driven (my aunt was hung as a witch in Connecticut). But my surgery has revealed a new, nefarious misspelling. Several of the comments to my recent Facebook posts addressed me as Mr. Belsen, and all of them came from mobile devices. Those Facebook friends have NEVER spelled my name wrong. So I would like to know what cell phone company has decided to autocorrect my family name to that of the most infamous Nazi concentration camp, and can I sue them?

Post-surgical observation #4:
And on the 10th day, he walked.

Arisen like some beefy red-headed Lazarus, imagining Gene Wilder standing over me, eyes rolled back, screaming "It's alive!!", I have returned to the world of the living with a vengeance.

Yesterday, I asked Helena if I could go shopping with her. Although she was reluctant to give up her tender ministrations that gave her unfettered access to my wallet in the other room, she assented. I needed another shower, hopefully with less sordid consequences than my first one. I took the organic Goo-Gone into the shower (yes, I am still sloughing off gunk from where the surgeon glued me to the table while he worked on my back), showered and shaved (amazing myself with a talent I haven't used since I was 18 years old), and got ready to meet the world once more.

We drove to the Acme supermarket, she rolled a shopping cart over to me to use instead of a walker, and what had once been the most mindless of activities became a voyage of wonder and discovery once again.

I visited the bakery and slavered over pecan pies I would never possess. I laughed with delight when my cart knocked over an orange display and all the fruit rolled everywhere in the produce department, necessitating a cleanup call. I demonstrated my weightlifting ability by hoisting a gallon of chocolate milk, which weighed eight pounds, pretty close to what I am allowed to lift, into the cart. For 25 minutes, I was an Oompa Loompa set free in Willie Wonka land.

But no matter what anyone else thought they were seeing, I knew that only 10 days earlier, a five minute walk in that same grocery would have resulted in me crumpling to the ground, unable to feel anything below my waist.

And on the way home we stopped at the new Dunkin' Donuts and got a toasted coconut beauty. I could get used to this.

Post-Surgery Observation # 5:
Lies my Surgeon Told Me, and other Fairy Tales

"This might be uncomfortable." - No, stubbing your toe is uncomfortable. Sharting before first period with a full schedule of classes and no replacement underpants in the top drawer of the file cabinet is uncomfortable. The first whiz after a man has had a catheter removed is NOT uncomfortable. It is like pissing razor blades. Just say so; it's going to happen either way, but don't lie about it.

"I don't know." - When I woke up from surgery, seven hours after I went under, I had four parallel scrape marks on my chest, which were deep enough that over the next few days they scabbed over. I asked the surgeon how that happened, and he said "I don't know." Now, I don't either, but the two possibilities that spring to mind are that my surgeon is actually Wolverine, and I got slashed during his metamorphosis, or one of his long-nailed nurses didn't appreciate my man-boob flopping over her sightlines during the surgery and batted it out of the way.

"This oxycodone prescription I'm giving you will cut the pain." - Yeah, it just might, if you hadn't given me SUGAR PILLS. I did a personal scientific study – I took the 5 mg tablet you gave me, then two hours later I ate about 10 M&Ms. The M&Ms made me feel better, so I finished the bag and felt great, Somehow, I don't think I'll have any problem weaning off the oxy; I'll have more trouble keeping the zombies from southern Portage County coming for the rest of those white sugar pills, plus convincing Helena that I really do need a giant size bag of M&Ms every night if she doesn't want to be awakened by my screams of pain.

Post-surgical observation #6

Sometimes good things come from misery. I gained 20 pounds when I quit using nicotine. In just 12 days of post-surgery (sounds like a Christmas carol coming on) I have lost all 20 pounds.

Further notes about the surgery: I had a very young nurse who applauded when I ripped my first fart after surgery. We need more of that kind of caregiver. And just in case you think I'm crass for typing that, every nurse who came through my room asked me if I had farted yet – apparently that's a sign of good things after surgery.

In the recovery room, I asked the surgeon how the surgery had gone. He said, "We had to make a couple deep cuts." Now, in my anesthetic haze, I expected to hear Rod Stewart singing "The First Cut is the Deepest." (Dr. Scot Miller was not the Cat Stevens version type, and it would have really freaked me out to hear Sheryl Crow in my head). But, nothing – no music of the spheres. It wasn't until a couple days later before I realize that what he REALLY said was doctor-speak for "You are one of the fattest people I ever had to plunge my hands into."

I had to wear electronic booties while I was in the hospital, which alternated squeezing each leg to prevent blood clots. While admirable in theory, they also used velcro straps that came loose the first night and latched on to the opposite boot, in effect becoming leg shackles. I called the night nurse and said somebody had come in and tied me up, for what reason I didn't know. She must have chalked it up to the drugs wearing off, because nobody ever came to rescue me. I eventually freed myself, and now feel that I could earn my Houdini Escape Badge in the Boy Scouts in my next lifetime.

When I got my first real shampoo, I was alarmed to see brown rivulets running out of my hair. As I worked the lather in, I felt two sore spots right above my ears. I asked Helena what they were, and she confessed that the doctor had said he had to screw a metal halo into my skull in order to maneuver me on the operating table. Between the holes in my head and the permanent tape/Super Glue gunk all over my body, I sure wish somebody had taken video of this old boy being flopped around like a tuna freshly pulled from the sea.

On the other hand, that's as close to a halo as I am likely to get in this lifetime or the next.

Post-surgical observations #7

I endured a tragicomic incident at the hospital the first day after surgery. I had just gone to the bathroom – the actual bathroom – for the first time since the surgery. I was pretty proud, having gotten most of it in the commode, and I ambled back out and sat in the wooden chair by the bed, which had a very comfortable plastic pillow seat. It was so comfortable, in fact, that I fell asleep for about half an hour, until Helena arrived. She woke me up, and I wanted to show her how I could cover the ten paces to the bathroom. I stood up to recreate my journey. That is when I learned that you don't sit on a plastic seat wearing only a backless hospital gown, as the seat was now firmly welded to the lowest hanging part of my body, swinging like a pendulum, and was more than willing to travel with me those entire 10 steps.

Fortunately, my wife, after laughing so hard she farted, took pity and broke the adhesive seal, but not before a significant amount of my tenderest skin had become a trophy of the war between a dazed and confused man and hospital furniture.

Helena being tied up elsewhere yesterday, the best friend the Beldens could have, Robert Geiser, volunteered to drive me to the podiatrist. Now, all the doctor does is take a Dremel (a power grinder) to rasp my claws down (I have given up calling them toenails) and stick pins into the bottom of my feet in search of the feeling I long ago surrendered to peripheral neuropathy (my grandkids used to play "This Little Piggy Went To Market" for hours and I never knew it). Well, the appointment was at 3:00, 20 minutes from home. We left at 2:00. Geiser and I got lost, driving around most of northern Ohio before finally arriving right on the dot at 3 PM. I could tell that Bob was exasperated at all the wrong turns; for myself, I told him he was pretty dumb for taking directions from somebody high on Oxycontin. It always helps to have an excuse.

Post-surgical observations #8

Very few of my students knew that Mr. Pop Culture, Mr. Beowulf, Mr. TV Director was also certified to teach – of all unlikely things – physical education. It would not have been pretty. So being the head volleyball and golf coach was as close as I ever came to using that certification.

And they certainly did not know that part of my phys ed certification was taking a class in ballet. Really. The old fat guy, 40 years ago, learned how to do the five basic positions, the grand battement, and an arabesque, and damned if I didn't earn an A in the class, to the horror of my emaciated 90 pound female classmates.

But of course I never used my ballet training, except that on occasion it made me more empathetic with my gay students, as if being a male English teacher hadn't already cast shadows on my entire career.

Until now. Since my lumbar fusion, I have been forbidden to stoop, slouch, bend over, twist, or otherwise deform my spine for several months. So that presents a problem: if I drop food on the floor, how can I retrieve it within the 5-second rule whereby I am still entitled to eat it?

The solution, dredged up decades later: the grand plié, a move I mastered in my ballet class. I don't have a picture of ME executing the move, but I present for your imagination and suspension of disbelief, George Belden preparing to pick up an M&M he dropped: notice how I scan the floor carefully while lowering myself, one arm flung in the air, back straight, heels together, knees pointed in opposite directions, making sure a grandchild or other rodent doesn't get it before me.

Post-surgical observation #9

Yesterday was graduation day, my 2 week post-op visit to the surgeon, and I passed with flying colors. But of course, the path to my diploma was anything but straight.

First of all, Helena had promised we could go out to lunch before the doctor's office, since I am getting sick of shredded wheat three meals a day (Helena has been kind of busy lately and couldn't cook her usual "meal of the week" which we eat for seven days straight, which was fine with me because it's usually pigs in a blanket, which offend pretty much every one of my five senses plus my imagination).

So we went to Red Lobster. That's when the universe decided to start playing jokes on the sad, fat old man with the walker.

Pushing said walker in the lobby of the Red Lobster, it got stuck on the seam between the carpet and the tiled foyer. Not a problem - this walker, a leftover from Helena's foot surgery four years ago, has developed a flat spot on one wheel, so that it occasionally acts like one of those supermarket carts with some disgusting blotchy thing stuck to one wheel. I was used to these rapid stops.

But combined with losing 20 pounds in two weeks, and wearing a bulky back brace, my sweat pants no longer hugged that area of my body where a waist would be on a normal sized person.

You probably know what happened next without any more description, but some of my students were, as I recall, a bit slow on the uptake. So what happened is, the jolt from the unexpected walker stop made me take a sudden breath - and my pants fell down. Too late to halt my momentum, I waddled into a full Red Lobster waiting area with my pants around my ankles, just glad that I had switched from Depends-sized tightie whities to boxers right before the surgery. And I was truly thankful for those boxers, or else the bug-eyed, aghast lunch patrons might have seen an honest to god red lobster. I tried to appear casual, as if this was the most natural thing in the world and I always walked around in my skivvies in the middle of winter, while Helena worked feverishly to get my pants back up before someone dialed 911.

We heard the waitresses drawing lots to see who would wait on us, and the loser, a chatterbox named Mary, tried to make conversation before taking our order, asking me if I always walked around with no pants, and was this a national craze among senior citizens. You get the idea. Our food appeared in record time, giving me the distinct impression they wanted us gone. We were as welcome there as feral pigs at a tea party, so we gobbled our food and even saved the ritualistic Belden belching for outside.

We drove over to the Crystal Clinic, registered, and got called back for the interview with a nurse's aide, Mia, who typed information into a computer. About two minutes into the interview, I stood up and asked Mia if she trusted me. Since Helena was in the room, I guess she felt safe and she said yes. I then announced that my weakened musculature no longer could hold in the volume of gas that I now generate (somebody could frack my ass and make a fortune), and that I really, sadly, apologetically, had to fart, but I was pretty sure it wouldn't smell. Now, it takes an ultimate act of patient/caregiver trust to stay in the room with a huge stranger who has just announced he is going to release noxious gases into an enclosed space. But bless her heart, Mia just said "Fire away" and stood there while a 30 second Gabriel's trumpet blast of wind rocked the walls. Mia smiled, but I looked in her eyes and saw terror. I hoped Helena appreciated what a gentleman I was to have taken Mia's feelings into consideration and offered her the chance to retreat, but the crimson shame on my wife's face told me differently.

Mia swiftly said "I think I have all the information I need" and passed me along to Katy, the physician's assistant who was going to be deciding my fate. Now, Katy is beautiful, truly gorgeous, and I told myself I would rather explode than to have her witness a scene such as Mia had endured, but that sort of crisis did not revisit us. She in fact invited me to drop my pants, an invitation a gentleman could hardly turn down, and looked at the serpent-like row of staples running up and down my spine. A few admiring utterances ("What a beautiful scar this will make!" and "That oozing from the bottom looks like a little teardrop, doesn't it?") and she decided that, rather than wait any longer, the 40 staples could come out. I did not see her take a special instrument, and I'm guessing she just took a nail file out of her purse and began popping them out one by one, with the same demeanor as one pops a juicy zit. Each staple hit the wall with a little ping, like the casings of a semi-automatic Glock softly dropping to earth during a gang shootout.

"Done," she told Helena. "You might want to sop up the blood from the staple holes for a few days." Helena retched her understanding of the instructions, Katy wrote a prescription for a disabled parking sticker, the only good thing to happen today, and we were on our way.

And now I have graduated. No longer bound to a walker with a flat spot on the wheel, I now have a four-legged cane that I can use to trip people surreptitiously while looking completely innocent. Life is getting better.

Post-surgical observation number 10

Lying on my back day after day in an improvised recovery room in a 130 year old house is giving me the screaming meemies. Once a day I drive to a grocery and wander up and down the aisles, pausing in the feminine products row long enough to attract the attention of store workers who wonder what kind of pervert the old guy reading the back of the douche package might be. Another fun game is to load up my cart with canned goods, and then put them back on the shelf exactly one product to the left or right. I'm a real fan of anarchy, as long as it's orderly.

But that still leaves 23 hours a day of the screaming meemies. Thank god for the horseflies.

Back in the fall, we had an invasion of fruit flies. First I put out fly stickum strips, which were effective but not a lot of fun, since a captured fruit fly can't move and just dies looking like a little statue. So next I put out saucers of red wine. The fruit flies drink the wine, get drunk, fall into the wine, swim around a little while, then drown, sinking invisibly to the bottom, out of sight. Then I discovered that when squadrons of fruit flies were on final approach to the wine saucers, I could stand there with a portable vacuum and suck them out of the air. It was great getting a dozen in a couple seconds, really pumping up the testosterone, but there was no sensory satisfaction in that.

Enter the Bug Zapper. I found it on Amazon. It looks like a tennis racket, uses AA batteries, and when you hold down the button, an electric current like a Taser flows through it. It's death on fruit flies, sending them to the great rotten fruit stand in the sky in an instant of blue magic and a very satisfying crackling sound. But it proved too efficient, eliminating several generations of fruit flies in a very few days, cutting short my fun just as winter approached.

Then I had surgery. Then I got stir crazy. And then the horseflies arrived. Huge hairy things with eyes the size of frozen peas and the intelligence of zombies, every year they show up in the tiny mud room attached to the side of our house, the carrion of a full season hanging from their legs like stalactites. Why they arrive at my house, like the buzzards of Hinckley, will have to remain a mystery of evolution. They have obviously spent the summer feasting on equine turds, and somehow believe they can treat my mud room as their spa as they overwinter, sharing gossip and getting fatter and lazier.

But they didn't reckon on the extremely bored fat guy with a chasm in his back armed with a lethal tennis racket. Oh, they're worthy adversaries. One swipe of the Zapper does NOT kill these filthy demons – it only pisses them off, like a red cape in front of a bull. They fall to the floor, crawl around for a little while, like dazed WWE grapplers regathering their strength, and attack again. A good healthy horsefly can get the shit zapped out of it four or five times until, like King Kong in chains, the fight is taken out of it.

At that point, as an act of mercy, I gently place the Zapper on top of my vanquished enemy and press the button. Instantly, little bolts of lightning fire off from each leg and wing tip, an aroma of terribly cooked liver permeates the mud room, and another gallant horsefly heads for its afterlife filled with manure and decaying flesh and probably thousands of unborn maggots.

And I have fought off my screaming meemies for a few more minutes.

Now I know that this activity is not gaining any karma points for me, that in fact those horseflies might be the reincarnation of former students who preceded me into the great Beyond, but I tell myself that Helena would be doing it if I wasn't, and she just sees flies as pains in the arse, instead of valiant warriors who have called upon me to assist them in their journey to Valhalla.

Post-Surgery Observations # 11:
Football and Grandchildren

Saturday was nirvana for a retired invalid who is stuck, by surgery and weather, in one room of a house where three other people live, three people who know they can escape my incessant bitching just by going upstairs, as I impotently flail my cane at them and sputter that they better come back and listen to my rantings, Yes, Saturday was nirvana because it was football, wall to wall, eyeball to eyeball, from one end of my sanitarium to the other, football, glorious football.

It started at 11 AM with the Division V Ohio state championship, featuring perennial finalist Coldwater, and ran through the Sportstime Ohio replay of the Mount Union-Wesley Division III college quarterfinals, which ended at 1:30 AM. Every single game, all day long, was a championship affair. I reveled in it. About once every quarter hour I screamed at Helena to come watch replays of incredible gridiron feats. And Saint Helena dutifully got out of her chair in the front room, where she had been watching a food show featuring dishes that will never grace the Belden table, stuck her head in my room, uttered a perfunctory "wow", and went back to her show. I tricked her once by telling her to "watch this replay" when it was actually an infomercial for a fake mouse under a hunk of cloth that is supposed to entertain your cat for years. She entered my room with glazed eyes, never looked at the screen, said "wow" and went out of the room again. I wonder what else she has been faking for our entire married life.

So anyway, if Saturday was a football orgasm, Sunday will probably be the erectile dysfunction of the week. And no, not because of the Cleveland Browns. Watching a Browns game has become the equivalent of the sign outside the Hell of Dante's *Inferno*: "Abandon hope, all ye who enter here." We Browns fans would be better off to order barbed wire scourges from Amazon, the better to flay the skin from our backs to take our mind off which 10th rate quarterback drafted from a Youtube video would be this week's sacrifice to a game the Browns can no longer play.

No, Sunday is the Slough of Despond for me because of one word: grandkids. Sniffling, slobbering, rasping, mucus-spewing, booger-eating, contagion-laden grandkids who are coming over today.

Am I the only grandfather who doted on each grandchild as he or she arrived, pretty close to one a year due to fertile daughters-in-law? Am I the only grandfather who passed along such tribal rites of passage as "pull my finger", who laughed and joyed when hearing their own precocious little toots even while they were still in diapers (well, for one of them, that stage lasted a tad too long for comfort....)

Am I the only grandfather whose unconditional love transformed into a nameless fear that his legacy, these last iterations of the power and magic of his loins, had become instead the agents of his death, sent by a dark power, using microbes to make him pay for a lifetime of debauchery – bound and determined to give me a disease that will cause me to cough so violently that my incision will be rent open, allowing my vital organs, my precious bodily fluids, to slither out of my almost-healed body?

These cunning little demons, my grandchildren, will come to pay tribute to their ill Papa, rubbing the edge of the quilt on my sickbed, wanting only to reach under the sheets and to stroke my wound with their diseased little digits, to finish me off completely.

And so my game plan for Sunday was finalized during the orgy of Saturday football. I will wear a surgical mask a la Michael Jackson, so they can't breathe their cooties on me. They will never know that I don't have a beard anymore and they wouldn't recognize me even if I took the mask off. If they attempt to sneak up and touch me, I have my four-pronged cane to fend off that attack. If they offer to bring me food, I'll make them taste it first to see if they die. And if by chance I survive this onslaught by my very own Grandchildren of the Corn, these vacant-eyed *Village of the Damned* imps who gather around to terrify me, I will tell you tomorrow that it was all a feverish dream – brought on by an overload of championship football the day before.

Post-Surgery Observations #12 – Taking Stock

I've always had some form of crutch to help create the persona I presented to the world. Back when I was a teacher and had to develop a cult of personality to disguise the fact that I was stealing money by being paid to teach things I would have done for free in a perfect world (history of rock and roll being the prime example), my crutch was a camera. I taught Television Journalism. I was the television man. I could walk into any classroom in the Maple Heights school system and instantly control that room. Kids would do whatever I wanted them to do, just because everyone wanted to be on television. 20 years of Maple students grew up knowing me, even if they did not have me as a teacher. Every teacher in the Maple system knew me, because I taught my television journalism students that there was a story happening every day in every classroom – we just had to find a way to tell it on camera. Teachers never knew when I might show up at their door unannounced looking for a story; they only knew that I wouldn't embarrass them .

When I retired in 2002, I had to reinvent myself. I'd spent the last 30 years in Maple Heights, where everybody knew me, some respected me, and a few even liked me, but not a single person in my hometown of Kent knew me. I'd won more state fair champion ribbons for growing vegetables than anyone in Kent history, but only my Maple kids knew about them, and they just thought it was another example of how weird I was (hell, for some of my students, my lectures on "Life Lessons We Can Learn from Squash" are the only things they remember about me).

So I bought a scooter. And I sat my prodigious butt on that scooter and rode around the Kent State University campus, waving to coeds. Sometimes I'd have a grandkid on the scooter with me, and I could actually hear the "awws" from the girls as they pointed at Santa on a Scooter and his little elf. So the scooter became my crutch – since I was basically irrelevant now, I at least had an object to keep me from becoming invisible.

But now, in this winter of transition from an active senior into a tired old man, I have to find another crutch, something else to say, hey, I'm not gone quite yet. And ironically, my new crutch is – a crutch! As I was doing my laps this morning at the grocery store, I realized that the cane that I use to keep my balance is like a wizard's wand, if I play my cards right. Everybody unconsciously defers to the handicapped – society breeds it into us, and it's the right thing to do – and my cane has bought me entrée into a new class of citizen. If I hobble up to a line with a few items of purchase, people let me go first. Cars stop, not just in crosswalks, but anywhere a cane is flashed. I'm still invisible – who cares about a fat old man limping through his golden years? – but for the length of time I will need it, the cane gives me a place in the world. After that, I'm on my own again. And Wednesday, when I start physical therapy, we'll start to see how that will work out.

Post-Surgery Observations #13
The Day From Hell

I didn't know that it would be the day from hell. I mean, when I woke up in my makeshift recovery room, it didn't smell any more sulfurous than usual, after Helena and I spend eight hours off-loading methane in our sleep (we always thought the kids had allergies because their eyes watered when they came into our bedroom, until we added 2 and 2 and started saving on the doctor bills). Apparently old Beelzebub hadn't visited overnight. So I had no idea that before the end of the day, I would be looking back over my shoulder to see if Charon, the boatman of the River Styx, had a searchlight out looking for the old guy with a hole in his back.

First, Helena had to run errands in the morning, so that left my son Garth to be the old man's shower room attendant for the first time. Now, anyone who meets him has no problem determining that he is MY son. He is damned near a clone. We don't have the same personality – Garth is more like Norm from Cheers. He can go into any bar in Kent and be greeted with a Greek chorus of "Garth! Garth's here!" Maidens throw themselves at his feet, something that never happened to me, so he must have got his mother's pheromones in the genetic swap.

Well, anyway, Garth is basically the same size as me, so the first visual treat for any ancient god happening to direct this Greek tragedy is two dancing bears, one completely naked, performing a fandango in a tiny bathroom, trying to finagle our way past each other with a minimum of fleshy contact so I can get to the shower. Once I was settled on the stool, I heard Garth's voice behind me, trembling with fear, asking "What part of you do I have to wash?" Now, I could have completely shattered the poor boy's mind with just a couple words related to uh-oh areas, but I allayed his anxieties by telling him that I was now able to wash every region myself, and his main responsibility was to make sure the old man didn't do a Humpty-Dumpty after his ablutions. Unfortunately, I am not able to DRY every region, so he had to make the sacrifice which no son should ever have to make. As I was getting dressed, I heard him washing his hands over and over, like Lady MacBeth, knowing that even if Garth scrubbed all his skin off, one cannot make things once seen, unseen.

So Helena returns, it's too cold to even consider walking outside, and I'm tired of walking at the grocery and seeing the same pitying looks on the stock-boys who nod at me as I walk by but roll their eyes when they think I'm not looking. I tell Helena I want to go someplace new to take my mind off my back, which right now feels like they drove the Golden Spike into my L5 vertebrae. She suggests I might enjoy dipping my toes into the latest in shabby chic, a tour of the Amish scratch and dent stores of Geauga County, where one can buy everyday goods for 10 cents on the dollar, as long as one is not too picky about what century the expiration date on them might be. This activity is big among retired teachers and Geauga County lawyers.

So OK, we go. But not taken into consideration is that George had dutifully swallowed his diuretic pill earlier, and Amish stores do not have indoor plumbing. So halfway through the first store visit I have to sneak outside, behind an Amish carriage, relieve myself, and prepare to blame the poor horse for the effluent mess clearly running between MY shoes. Then I go back inside to see Helena waving a box of raisin bread mix at me. "39 cents!", she enthuses, knowing that I love raisin bread and hoping this will give her a few more credits toward sainthood, being both cheap and pleasing to her man. I'm happy for her – until I see the name of the brand, one I am not familiar with: Krusteaz.

Later I will learn that Krusteaz is a respected baking label from Continental Mills. However, at that precise moment all I see is a name I have never seen before, so, using my decades of training, I sound it out: Crus-ty-ass. My wife wants me to eat Crusty-ass bread!

Shoving aside innocent lasses in long dresses, John Lennon glasses and bonnets, I dash for the car as fast as my cane will allow me. Helena must have thought I had to pee again, but no, I now recognized her for the Lucrezia Borgia she really is, determined to poison me in the name of love. And that, my friends, is a mere slice of my day from hell. There is much more to tell, but I am afraid your mind cannot withstand the sheer torment, so I will be your firewall from the horror, the horror, the horror of it all..

Post-Surgery Observations #14
The Saga of the Blue Recovery Room

We own a 130 year old house. Unless you have ever lived in a house built circa 1880, with a plaque from the local historical society on the front detailing the entire history of the building, which still has its original plumbing and radiator heating system complete with a boiler in the basement (which basement was blasted into the bedrock of the old Cuyahoga River channel and has never leaked) – I say unless you have been the caretaker of such a structure, it would be hard for you to imagine having to face a radical change in your house at the same time you are facing 6 to 12 months of incapacitation.

Well, I have.

It was 6 months ago that I began to surrender my ability to walk to progressive spinal stenosis. It was just about that same time that the ceiling began to fall in the central area we call the Blue Room for the color of its wallpaper.

Oh, we knew it was going to fall when we moved in 25 years ago. The ceiling had a lot of cracks in its original plaster, but we could see that one area had been patched – the outline was visible in bumpy plastering. We determined that it was underneath the vanity in the upstairs bathroom, which had probably leaked, weakening the plaster in that spot below. For the past quarter century, we had witnessed the glacial progression of the cracks around the patch. We put a daybed underneath it for when my mother-in-law visited, and I never verbalized my hopes that her heavy snoring might hasten the collapse.

No, the damned plaster kept hanging on, the cracks widening until you could actually see the lath-work underneath, until the very day that an MRI determined that my spine channel had so narrowed it was choking off everything below my waist, and I was scheduled for the first available open-spine surgery, one month off.

Then it decided to fall.

This was the room that was going to be my post-op recovery room, so we had to work quickly. I wanted to bring in an expert plasterer to repair it immediately, but Helena "knew a guy." Since Helena always wins, the "guy" came in, and gave us two options: patch the hole, or clean out that area and then place drywall over the entire 350 square feet of this enormous ceiling.

Need I tell you which option Helena chose?

So her "guy" tore down a large area of ceiling, and in the process revealed not only rotten lath-work, but cascaded 130 year old dust down onto the entire room. Garth, Helena and George, all being highly allergic, immediately came down with the galloping miseries for 10 days, wheezing and gasping through surgical masks while the "guy" worked. And as Helena gazed up through the hole into the bathroom above, she was struck with a wonderful idea. As long as we were doing the ceiling below it, let's also redo the entire bathroom above it!

So, we call in the plumbers (professionals, whom I have used often), intending to install a new vanity and toilet, leaving the original clawfoot tub in place. The plumbers declare that our galvanized pipe is unusable, and install all new plumbing up through the wall from the basement to the upstairs bathroom. Only it wouldn't fish through the wall – which means they had to cut a huge 3 foot wide strip from ceiling to floor in the wall to guide the new pipes. Which means we now had to redo not only the entire ceiling, but the entire wall, which had been wallpapered 25 years ago.

Helena now decides that of course we need a new floor in the upstairs bathroom. Her "guy" knows another "guy" who does tile.

So, the upstairs bathroom is completely remodeled, the downstairs ceiling is completely drywalled but needs painted, and the entire blue room needs either repainted or re-wallpapered.

Garth knows a "guy" who hangs out at the bar with him and knows how to paint. Helena thinks this "guy" will do just fine. In five days I will be lying under this ceiling, next to these walls, with my wife and my heavy-hipped son taking dumps over my head into the new untested toilet, and all I have between me and 130 years of dust and mold in my open wound are some "guys" who hang around Kent bars.

So Garth's "bar guy" paints the ceiling, primes the walls, and we are left stranded: there is no time left , and the contents of the blue room, which includes my huge record album collection and other debris from my former life, are scattered in every other room of the house. The house is, to be blunt, a fu**ing mess. The wallpapering or painting – undecided as yet – will have to be put off until January, when I am recovered enough to move back to my old room.

So I lie here, surrounded by the sorry saga of the blue room: unpainted but primed walls, a daybed, a recliner I am forbidden to use by my surgeon, a television, a card table and straight back chair for the few hours I feel strong enough to tap away on my laptop – and this is the environment from which these past few weeks of status updates have been generated for you to enjoy, to take my mind off the sorrowful situation I find myself in.

Oh, and the ceiling "guy", the tile "guy", and the barfly painter "guy"? I'd recommend them in a minute. Every one of them did a stunning job at a third of what I expected to pay. Maybe Helena's good fortune will carry through to my recovery. We'll find out – physical therapy begins today, and I may not be writing so much. Gotta save some time for myself.

The Beldens Go To Great Britain 2000

We're in Kilkenny Ireland on a lunch stop. The bus ride has proven somewhat ambivalent; George and Helena both seem to fall asleep as soon as the bus starts and miss much of the commentary. This might have something to do with how many different brands of hard cider we feel a compulsion to sample every night.

We finally got a good night's sleep last night in a hotel next to Trinity College in Dublin, after what felt like five nights in the Tower of London's dungeon, since our last hotel had beds like rocks. One of Ireland's two canals ran 10 yards from the door, so George, the canal buff,was happy. We watched England lose in the Euro 2000 soccer matches, which made the Irish joyful. We visited a cricket game; the pub owner later said it must have been Protestants, because they were the only ones who played that "posh" game in Ireland.

The flight from London was fine, except that we were on Ryan Air, a cheapo outfit that charged for water and to use the loo on the plane. We have hooked up with a group of people from the other side of the world – New Zealand sheep farmers - and a family from Garfield Heights, very near to where George teaches in Maple Heights. We went on a panorama tour of Dublin last night, with a heavy emphasis on literary points. Our tour director seems to be an Oscar Wilde fan; she characterized him as a "poor misunderstood boy who still managed to father two lovely children." She is the mistress of euphemisms.

We motored to the Irish National Stud farm this morning; one stallion put on quite a show for Helena, but that's another story.

Part Two

Sorry if these messages are kind of cryptic, but we are being charged £1 per 8 minutes for internet time on the slowest Apple computer that God ever invented.

We are in Kenmare, on the southwest coast of Ireland, near Killarny. It is the most rugged hunk of land we have ever seen, yet there are sheep by the thousands on the top of every mountain. This is a special breed that stays outdoors all year round. They have stripes on their side to show how many times they've been mated. It's a good thing they don't do that to the girls George is teaching. Some of them would look like zebras.

We went to Blarney yesterday to kiss the stone. Nobody told us it was at the top of a damned castle. 126 steps up a narrow medieval passageway with your nose crammed in the butt of the person ahead of you. 60 minutes to climb up, 10 seconds to jam your lips where 10 million have slobbered before, and 45 seconds down a separate narrow passage with a rope to hang on in case you fall.

Helena did everything the traditional way, but George forgot to push AWAY from the rock (you lay on your back and hang over a precipice to do the deed) and instead rose straight up, so instead of kissing the Blarney Stone, he bled all over it, which grossed out the German tourists behind us, and they began to curse us, not knowing that Helena was born in Germany and knew everything they were spitting out.

We've been eating muesli every morning, which has kept us very regular. Helena has been more continent than most, and gassed a hapless New Zealander behind her at the hotel. The poor Kiwi just wanted to help her with her room key. That will be the last gesture of goodwill from the southern hemisphere for a long time, since Helena's southern hemisphere spoke volumes.

Part 3

We are in Stratford-On-Avon, and we are checking the shops closely. I want to replace my willie with one with a wooden head. In case you haven't figured it out, I'm looking in the tourist shops for a wooden statue of Shakespeare to replace the plaster one which a freshman fondled too lovingly last year and dropped on the floor of Room 211.

We flew into England yesterday, after one too many days in Ireland. "Danny Boy" caused me to convulse about the 90th time I heard it, but it's great for the tourist industry, since everyone wants to get drunk to avoid thinking about the NEXT time someone will sing it (about 10 minutes later, usually). Our tour director fell asleep between Limerick and Dublin and left the same tape looping in the cassette deck, so I can now sing every one of the seven songs the Irish ever wrote.

We rented a car at Gatwick and headed west on the M freeways. I thought I was doing great until I noticed the 16 wheel lorry headed right at me, and realized I had inadvertently drifted onto the Yankee side of the road. My lusty scream probably registered with the locals as just another bad rendition of "Too Ra Loo Rah Loo Rah". Speaking of which, I had to go to the loo right after that, but that's the rental agency's problem.

No pedestrian has had the stupidity to step in front of me, so I've done quite well. I've discovered Helena has lost ability to read signs more than five meters from her face, so she's no help as a navigator and has taken to sleeping 20 hours at a stretch. She says she trusts me.

We stayed in Woodstock last night above a pub - how convenient for our current lifestyle - and drove all of 30 miles today before stopping in Chipping Campden, a local market town that happened to have two quilt stores which Helena immediately moved into with no intention of ever leaving. So we decided to take a room there, again above a pub (naturally). It's a good thing quilt stores don't serve cider, or Helena would never come home. Tomorrow we're heading off for Wales.

Part 4

We traveled though several lovely little English market towns: Chipping Campden, Ludlow and Stretten Church, which had some nice antiques.

From there we decided to go to Wales, and headed back to a place our sons will remember from our trip in 1990, Llangollen. This time we picked an in-town rat hole above a pub to stay in. We should have known better when the cost was only £26 for a double, and there was no one else in the place. In fact, there had been no lodgers for several centuries, as far as I can tell.

The TV didn't work (on the night of the France-Portugal Euro 2000 soccer showdown, damn it.) so we had to read in the sitting room, which was filled with the detritus of long-departed Edwardian visitors. Candies not manufactured in the last half-century were discovered in the creases of the sitting room chairs, and Helena ate them anyway, due to her chocaholism (as dramatic and sad as her cider fetish).

During our last visit to Llangollen, a sheep stuck its head in the drawing room of the bed and breakfast at which we were staying. This time, at the *Hotel du Rodent*, I was awakened to the pleasant sight of a pigeon pooping on our open window sill, directly on the hem of the shirt I had hung there to block out some of the noise from the yobs celebrating France's disgraceful soccer win.

Then, and Helena doesn't know this, I had to chase a spider the size of a silver dollar from the coffin-like shower stall before I could generate the piss-stream of water that we got for the £26 tariff.

We soon discovered that the barmaid had locked us in after closing shop so that we wouldn't go downstairs and raid the taps. I guess the legends of Helena's cider consumption were preceding us across the country. So the denizens of Wales were treated to the sight of two old, overweight Americans squeezing out a window and climbing down a rickety fire escape with all their luggage.

Sam and Garth will remember their mother's antics in our next city of Chester 10 years ago, which she claims not to remember, but as I recall involved the words "pull my finger" with a Cornishman. Well, anyway, we are much more prim and proper this time, and have taken a walking tour of the entire town via self-directed map. We didn't know, 10 years ago, that one can walk the entire circuit of this walled Roman town, on top of the wall. It is really the best tourist thing to do outside of London. We got to see the Bridge of Sighs, which was the name of a Robin Trower album, and now we know what it means. It's about two feet wide, crosses the Shropshire Union canal at a height of about 50 feet, and was the footbridge condemned prisoners walked. The bridge was so narrow that any attempt to rescue them would result in their death, as well as the rescuers, in a rather precipitous fall.

We are planning to head north to Lancaster this afternoon, as the staging area for a full day in the Lake district on Friday. We figured Grasmere and Windermere would be pretty bad on the weekend for finding a place to stay, so we will start working our way to Nottinghamshire after that.

Part 5

From Chester we went to the Lake District, and actually became tourists there, taking a long cruise on the middle of Lake Windermere, and walking though the town of Ambleside, where I bought a 100 year monograph about Dante Gabriel Rossetti at a paper show for £3. Then it was onto the M roads for a lengthy drive at 95 MPH to get to Scotland.

Friday night was a horror. Every place we stopped in the south of Scotland, about 50 miles south of Edinburgh, had the same story. We would go into pubs and inns, ask if they had a room, and they recoiled as if we were lepers, crossing their fingers and chanting "jimclark, jimclark" at us. We thought it was an exorcism for ugly foreigners or something.

Finally, we asked one desk clerk what "jimclark" was, and it turns out to be a massive Scottish road race like the Cannonball Run, and we were right in the midst of it. Every room in Scotland was booked. So finally, drinking away our sorrows and wondering what field to sleep in, a fellow who owned a bed and breakfast next door was tippling with us, and he turned out to have a spare room, so we had lodgings in a old converted sheep shed. Any manger in an emergency....

We have driven up to Edinburgh, are taking the city tour, and jumped off when we saw this internet cafe. We're heading to Yorkshire tomorrow as we start back toward Gatwick.

Part 6

Edinburgh was the last message. The weather has finally turned miserable, making the drive ghastly but appropriate. We decided to head down to the Yorkshire moors, but since the fog prevented seeing more than 10 feet in front of us, and the roads are the Roman roads less than two cars in width with hairpin curves every two feet or so, we felt much closer to the dead people in the Bronte novels.

The weather cleared up a bit, so we decided to visit Hadrian's Wall, built in 100 AD across the entire island by Emperor Hadrian to keep out the Picts of the north, who had the nasty habit of eating Roman hearts when they were able to rip them out. That was probably the most meaningful historical stop of the trip. We got some great pictures of the wall, most of which still stands, but one really couldn't tell Hadrian's from any of the 10000 other sheep walls unless you knew what you were looking for.

We had another horrible night trying to find a place to say. Helena loves living on the edge, but the muesli I eat every morning makes my nervousness much more vivid. We finally got a hotel/pub room in Hexham, which is the trollop capital of Yorkshire, because when we went for our nightly stroll, every female above the age of eight was tricked out in gallons of perfume, with troweled-on makeup, trolling the street for the toothless, tattooed yobs who seem to constitute the majority of the English populace.

There was an Italian restaurant on the second floor of a building, where the local dirty old men hang out looking down the blouses of the trollops. This seems to be a local tradition, since the girls stop and wiggle their tits at the gents, who applaud and hold up fingers to indicate a "whore score." It made interesting viewing. Our room was nicer than sleeping in the streets which were littered with condoms, so we were happy.

Yesterday we visited a medieval faire at Middleham, which has a great ruined castle, the childhood home of Richard III. Even though he was the most vile king in English history, they seem quite proud of him, like a local boy made good. I guess it would be the same as if Revere High School in Ohio erected a monument to Jeffrey Dahmer for his world-famous achievements.

We have wended our way just south of Cambridge for the night; it's 2 pm and we already have a room in the lovely town of Saffron Walden. Is that a great name or what? And having an internet cafe in this burg is beyond belief. Our room has a definite medieval ambiance: the room tilts about 30 degrees from one end to another, the bathroom is timbered a la Stan Hywet in Akron, and there is a definite aroma of ancient wattle and dung coming from the plaster. Can't beat that for living the history, eh?

The Beldens Go To England 2003

Blimey, mates! At the risk of mixing cultures and languages, The Beldens made it back to the motherland once again. George is in absolute heaven, ready to die, because we got tickets for *My Fair Lady* last night, at the original Drury Lane theater where it not only had its very first performance 50 years ago, but the action of the play is actually set outside the theater, so we could leave the performance and see the actual sites that inspired Shaw when he wrote *Pygmalion* in 1911. It was the most incredible stage production George had ever seen, and he has seen at least 30 productions of *My Fair Lady*.

We also attended a matinee of the Reduced Shakespeare Company production of *Shakespeare Abridged* - 37 plays in 97 minutes. We had front row center, and both of us became part of the play (especially Helena, whose hearty cider-enhanced chortle became a running theme of the actors' improvisations).

The flight over was a vacation in itself. Right across the aisle from George was a young twenty-something with a body of mythological proportions, the physique of Aphrodite. Unfortunately, she had the face of a Gorgon (think John Elway if you are myth-impaired) and the morals of a satyress. She was accompanied by a lout who drank 12 airline bottles of vodka in three hours, talking loudly the whole time and groping her, and then thankfully he fell into a coma, which is when the show began. As soon as she felt his drool on her shoulder, she spread a blanket over her waist and began to, and there is no other way to say this (so parents get your children away from the book or Kindle), she began to pleasure herself. Slowly at first, so that we did a double, triple, and for George, octuple take, and then faster and faster. We were afraid the vibrations would bring the plane down, and Helena could not take notes fast enough, but after awhile this stupid creature forgot what she was doing and fell asleep. George did not notice if she washed her hands afterward. So George did not sleep on the flight. Helena did, but only after spreading a blanket on herself and beginning some weird hand motions.

When we arrived we had several hours to waste, so we boarded a double decker and proceeded to fall asleep on the top deck in about five minutes. George slumped forward and woke up staring at a very angry Middle Eastern man who regarded George's mouth on his wife's burka-covered head as an affront. Helena was snapping pictures the whole time, and George had to gracefully back out of situation by pretending to be amnesiac and not knowing where he was.

The hotel was great. The manager took one look at George and Helena and discovered a room with four beds that could be shoved together to make one big enough to hold them. The Beldens thought that was just peachy. We are now on our way to Gatwick to pick up a car and drive to Jane Austen's birthplace to begin our real vacation. We went to the National Portrait Gallery yesterday to see the only picture of Jane known to exist. A niece of hers once said it was "a nice portrait", meaning she was as ugly as hell, I guess. Anyway, she can't be any uglier than the masturbating woman on the plane, so bring her on.

We gotta go. The internet cafe clerk yelled at us to clean the chocolate off the keys after Helena typed an email to our sons. Yes, fans, she has resumed her habit of carrying a brick of the brown stuff around to gnaw at frequent intervals.

Part 2

I'm writing this from a public library in Exeter with a time limit on the computer use, so I have to hurry.

We stayed the first night out of London in Winchester; old timers will remember the song "Winchester Cathedral." We stayed above a pub right across the street from that church. We were serenaded all night long by the sound of drunks puking in the street. The pub closed at 11:30 but several yobs apparently decided to eat bad fish with their bad teeth, making the alcohol and the cod come right back up. There were lots of young trollops on the streets. This is a British tradition, as we saw it last time we were in England, too.

George did not sleep a wink, which gave him time to discover all the used latex objects hidden under the mattress. Helena slept like a log.

The next day, Saturday, we spent in Bath, a wonderful town of sandstone - 7000 exactly identical sandstone houses which made getting around such a treat. The tour director kept pointing out a different historic house that looked exactly like the last one. George thinks all the events occurred in one house and the bus just kept going around the block. We spent the night in a great hotel built by first betting pool winner in England.

We then drove to Cerne Abbas, where we saw a chalk carving in a mountainside of a giant man with even more gigantic genitalia, kind of like Viagra during the Julius Caesar era. E tu, you brute! The locals are quite proud that their chalk carving has the biggest dick in the kingdom.

The next stop was Dorchester and Thomas Hardy country. Those folks are proud of public hangings, friends. They even had plaster casts of the heads of hung people. Called them art. No wonder all of Hardy's heroines killed themselves.

Last night we slept in a seaside resort named Lyme Regis, in a fantastic old hotel called the Mariner that overlooked the Cobb, the slip of harbor featured by local boy John Fowles in his book, *French Lieutenant's Woman*.

Helena now has a chunk of chocolate the size of a cement block to gnaw on, and has bought a bottle of cider to while away the few moments between pub visits. She's a different woman on the road, folks.

The best town we went through: Buttclose. The best pub name: The Blue Balls.

There are fewer internet cafes this time around. WiFi and laptops are slowly conquering England. But we'll keep trying to keep in touch. Actually, we need a laundry much more than the internet right now. Dirty clothes fill the back seat, which has the side benefit of keeping locals from prying too closely.

Part 3

This email comes hard on the heels of the last one because we found an internet cafe in Plymouth, and jumped off the bus. Our guide wasn't with us; he had slipped off the bus and was drunk. The driver was giving us a "silent tour" while he searched the streets for the guide.

We spent last night on a farm bed and breakfast outside of Plymouth, with nothing special but a non-flushing toilet. There was a good pub down the road so George was nearly tempted to test his drunk-driving skills for the first time, but fought off the urge. We were served breakfast by a woman who looked like June Cleaver from *Leave It To Beaver*, if June had a French/Cornish accent and had been a war bride of WWII vintage.

Exeter was boring really, except for the toilet. Every little village has public "facilities" - I think it's a law - and Exeter had a decent one, BUT George found an open "baby-changing" loo that needed a key from a shopkeeper, but was somehow unlocked. In he goes to a very fine, clean toilet, but the door locked behind him and he had to spend five minutes beating on the door, until a young kid yelled to his mummy that there was a baby locked in the washroom, and George was ignominiously rescued. He did not chat with his rescuers. Helena was eating strawberries at a market, oblivious to George's plight.

We now have seen a Blue Peter pub to go with the Blue Balls.

Part 4

We stayed in a place called Polzeath, in southwest Cornwall near England's bottom left corner, which is the only beach in England where one can surf. It was amazing; we parked on the beach and watched the surfers until 10 PM. The place we rented was an efficiency apartment that overlooked the bay. It had a wonderful view, but the only problem is that we had to pay extra for electricity. We had to crawl under the sink and put a pound coin in a slot for electricity for the night. That's a first. We got drunk to celebrate finding that British oddity. We found a new cider called Scrumpy Jack, which has become Helena's new nickname.

Getting to Tintagel, supposedly the site of King Arthur's conception, was all narrow winding roads with sharp rocks on either side. Helena enjoyed the view, while George held his breath all the way. The path down to Tintagel was very steep and walking back up was rough. We could have gotten a Land Rover ride up for one pound but were too proud to do it, so our legs ached for two days. The view was incredible. Tintagel Castle is on an island with access from a connecting bridge. As I said, King Arthur was supposedly born here. It's a lie, but the British milk it for all they can. The windswept ocean view would be enough of a tourist sell.

We next drove to to Cardiff, a nice enough town if you like coal. There's nothing older than 150 years, and everything was financed on the back of Welsh coal miners. The docks are being renovated like Baltimore's Inner Harbor. We went to Cardiff Castle only to ask where restroom was. Helena occupied the guard's attention while George sneaked in to the loo. We were the only ones dumb enough to take the double decker tour that rainy day.

We stumbled onto a small town named Usk in Wales for the night, the first of two Castle Inns in which we stayed. It's a nice town but nothing special. Then we drove to Much Wenlock, chosen by us for its name. There we discovered a weird local tradition called "well dressing", which involves dressing up a local well in flowers and baked clay tablets. There is no American tradition to compare it to. They think it's hot stuff, but it just looks stupid, since the wells have been dry for 700 years. It's like blessing the turds at a local sewage disposal plant, I guess.

Shrewsbury is a fine little Tudor town where we spent lots of time, and then to Buxton in the middle of the Peaks District National Park. Traffic was so horrible that we panicked and kept going, ending up in the county of Derby in a little town called Bakewell . Helena found a quilt shop and thought she'd died and gone to heaven. George fell asleep while waiting, so he enjoyed it too. We stayed at another Castle Inn, where six Americans from the University of Michigan got drunk and destroyed half the town. Stupid yobs. George wanted to toss a pisspot from the window on them. We had breakfast in a shop that sold the Bakewell Pies, one of England's most famous traditions. If you take every sweet substance on earth and toss them together, and then spread clotted cream, whipped cream, custard, and strawberry jam on the top, that will give you an idea. And clotted cream is not nearly as gross as it sounds.

A bartender said it was good thing we didn't stay in Buxton - the town is full of pickpockets and thieves. Of course, he admitted he'd never been there, though it is only 12 miles away. He warned us about Matlock, too, which is where we are typing this, at the local library. The librarian is eyeing Helena's purse, so she's probably one of those thieves he warned us about.

Part 5

We've made it to Yorkshire, as far north as we plan to go. We are in a very small town in the middle of the moors, named Malton. It is a lovely town; we stayed in a three-star hotel, we have shopped the Saturday market, gone to an arts and crafts fair, taken a two mile city hike, and it is still only 9:30 AM. We are sharing a cyber cafe with several 12 year olds who treat this like a Chucky Cheese and irritate the hell out of us.

We visited Monsal Head, one of the most incredible vistas in the country; it's a gorge carved by the River Wye (from Wordsworth's *Tintern Abbey,* for all the English majors reading this). We drove about 20 miles of very narrow road along the crests of England's highest hills, followed by about 4000 motorcyclists headed for England's biggest rally. There is a concert near here by a long-forgotten group named Status Quo that is the biggest thing to happen locally in recent years.

As last night was Friday we were treated to the traditional trollop parade that seems to be endemic everywhere in England. These were not so stinky, perfume-wise, and not nearly so clothes-fashionable as we have encountered elsewhere, but they were whores nonetheless.

We went drinking, at several places in fact, and found out that Anthony (Emptyhead) Greenwood has been banned from the pubs until 2007. His name and several others are posted above the entrance of every pub. This lout cannot hold his liquor - he is called Emptyhead because he uses the brain cavity to store his booze. The barmaid said he would never really be allowed to drink in a pub again, which means we will unfortunately never actually get to meet a man named Emptyhead.

We met three local lads in the pub who wanted to know everything about America. I talked to the intellectual of the group, while Helena has earned the right to call the other two "mate" (nudge, nudge, wink, wink). The one who wants only to be either a safari leader or veterinarian is saving money for university, although he really needs a dentist more, and the Scotsman who wants to be an elementary teacher seems to be equipped to deal with ten year olds, since that was the level of his discussion. My intellectual discussion companion only wanted a girlfriend, as he is tired of being a virgin.

Part 6

Hi again! Only a few days to go and much closer to home. We spent the day in York and did an awful lot of street walking in narrow alleys. We saw our first fist fight, between two idiotic teenagers, with lots of blood, and then got to see some Morris Dancers (old men in dresses trying to stab each other while doing weird posturing).

Well, since we missed Beverley (they were having a folk festival and there were no rooms) we headed to the North Sea. We found a marvelous place called the Marine Hotel in Hornsea, with the winds howling, ancient Viking spirits in the air, and 15 damned children in the room next to ours. They played outside until almost midnight in the rain, and then came inside for some wall soccer. George did not sleep that night. The pillows were like postcards with linen sewed on. But it was only 30 pounds so might have been worth it. Helena sleeps through everything, thanks to Tylenol PM and nightly chocolate overdose.

We then drove to Newark on Trent for no apparent reason, but it turned out to be a wonderful choice. We had a personal guided tour of the castle where King John of Magna Carta fame died in 1216. Poisoned, they say. Helena said she could still smell his corpse in the room, which offended the guide, named Derrek, who couldn't smell the mold because he chainsmoked through the tour. Anyway, we found out that Newark was the last Royalist stronghold during the Civil War, and that Charles I had fled 7000 Scottish troops only to surrender the next day at a pub in Southwell named the Saracen's Head, which still exists.

Well, that decided where we would spend lunchtime. George just had to have a pint in the very pub where England's only executed monarch had spent his last night of freedom. So we drove five miles to Saracen's Head and had a brie cheese sandwich that was so good Helena cried with delight and declared we had to stay there, so she could have one for dinner too. It turned out to be a three-star accommodation that housed not only Charles I but the Beatles, too, so it was well worth the cost.

We went to visit The Workhouse, a former asylum for the poor and "addle-brained." Only in England would this be a tourist attraction. We were invited to pretend we were poor and destitute and beg for admission at the gate, where a tourist guide would decide our fate. I am not making this up.

Last evening we got to see a gala parade of the British Legion through the streets of Southwell for a memorial service at the grandest Norman cathedral in England. The British Legion is like the American Legion except they don't get drunk until after the parade. They wear dresses too, or maybe they were kilts. Knobby knees are knobby knees on 80 year old men. Still, it was elegant - we took lots of pix, and mingled with the lads at the pub after.

Today Helena got to go to a quilt shop in the prison where Charles I was held until his execution. Helena wants to point out it is technically a castle, but that's only to justify the three hours we drove around on weed-infested cartpaths trying to find the damned place.

We jumped off a tour bus in Cambridge when we saw this internet cafe, and we'll jump back on when done. We're heading in the general direction of Dover next, and thence to Gatwick, where we will stay Wednesday night. And then it's back to the USA, and the end of another fantastic visit to the British Isles.

The Beldens Go To England 2006

Hi! George and Helena Belden, and Robert K. (no one knows what it stands for) Geiser are heading for the United Kingdom! We can't say for sure that we will be checking in every day (as none of us is bright enough to use WiFi, which is ubiquitous in England and thus labels us very slow technologically), but we will make every effort to get on-line at an internet café every third day, at least. Internet cafés sell chocolate, so Helena is able to locate them by smell alone. Her entire face quivers near chocolate, kind of like a witching stick, once we leave the shores of the United States.

This will be Geiser's first trip to the UK. I told him not to bother with a haircut or toothbrush, as things like dental hygiene would make him conspicuous as an outlander in England. He has also lost a little weight, so as to not be labeled "Meester Big Belly," as he was by a Costa Rican urchin on our last trip. And this is while he was standing right next to your chubby writer, who was given the nickname "Meester Whiskas."

We will try to keep you abreast of the adventures we are having. Depending on how much alcohol we have consumed that day in the form of Guinness, hard cider, mead, or Irish whiskey, the emails may not be intelligible, but you will at least know we have survived another day of driving on the wrong side of the road.

Our itinerary takes us to London for five days, and then on the road to discover the heart of England and Wales for seven days. What we have planned currently is to move in a clockwise fashion from Gatwick Airport, in the south of England. Our first stop may well be Brighton, which we have never visited. Helena wants to go to Cornwall again, we want to hit Wales, I want to go to Chester and York, but as always, the last pub we hit on any given day, and the friendly advice of local tipplers (or louts, yobs, punters, or wankers in a crunch), will be our guide to the next day's adventures.

Following that, we return our hopefully intact automobile to Gatwick for a flight to Scotland, where we join a bus tour of that magic kingdom. Geiser already has a list of every distillery in the country, and has taken a solemn vow to sample anything put in front of him. You might want to look up *haggis* to see how I plan to test his veracity.

From Edinburgh, we will again hit the air to Dublin to join a bus tour of the Emerald Isle. Helena did not schedule Ryan Air Lines this time, as they charge to use the bathroom on board. Bob and Helena will have to develop cat-like reflexes to keep me from throttling anyone who sings "Danny Boy" more than twice in a 10 minute span. And since this perversion seems to be innate in every Irishman, I may be spending the rest of my life in an Irish gaol, much like Oscar Wilde did (although his "crimes" were of a more, uh, intimate nature than strangulation). The tour ends in Shannon, from whence, if we are alive and still speaking to each other, we depart for home.

Part 2

Hello all! We are now four days into our trip, and aside from have feet swollen to the size of pillows, and fermented breath that could melt the heart of any Irishman, we are doing fine.

The plane trip was as uneventful as one could imagine. The transatlantic trip was only half full, so everyone got to spread out in the seats. Of course, George spreads out wherever he sits, so Helena was relieved of the burden of having his flesh oozing over into her seat. The meal was chicken, which was truly dreadful. George asked the stewardess if it had been purchased when they began killing flocks in the UK due to the bird flu outbreak, or if it was left over from the 1967 culling. She didn't appreciate that. We arrived at Gatwick at 6:30 AM and made our way to our hotel, which sits literally in the center of London. It's called the Charing Cross Thistle, and the famous Charing Cross sits five yards from the front door. It is a huge 12th century monument from which all distances in the UK to London are measured. Rooms are relatively huge, and a bargain at $220 a night.

Since it was now only 9 AM., we left the bags at the hotel and jumped on the double decker bus tour of London, hop on hop off. We had various narrators when we got on again. One we named the Mumbler, and the other was the Pisser as he bragged about every bridge he had urinated from as we passed under it.

Part of the tour was a trip by boat up the Thames. Now, as background info, George had been visiting doctors all week before departure, to prevent having his toe amputated (long story), so he is on a cocktail of antibiotics which play havoc with the stomach. The trip on the Thames proved to be too much, and George puked into the drinking water of 7.8 million Brits. He felt much better, but it did not help the ugly American image. Helena and Bob decided to have their first drink of the trip to celebrate George's return to his normal self. After that, they drank again, making fun of George because he isn't allowed to drink while on the antibiotics.

That night we roamed around Trafalgar Square, which is only about a half a block from us. There was an Indian music festival, which made Bob's butt twitchy. George thought he was dancing, but he actually had to find a loo really quickly, so they ended up going to the National Art Gallery. Most people go there to see the da Vinci's, but not the Beldens. It was an 8:30 bedtime after 48 hours awake.

George got up at 6 AM the next morning to a miraculous sight. Stumbling out of the hotel, he walked down a side alley and was accosted by many naked teenage girls, or at least they appeared that way to an old man. It turns out that this day was a bank holiday and all the clubs had stayed open till 6 AM, and the young ones had just arrived home on the Tube (our hotel sits over Charing Cross station). It was raining, George had an umbrella, and he mistook their stares for lust. One approached with money in her hand; George almost had a heart attack, but she just wanted to buy the umbrella from him.

When Helena and Bob got up we looked for breakfast but everything was closed, so we ended up eating at the hotel, and paid $28 for a continental breakfast. We did end up stuffing our pockets with fruit and muesli, but that was a bit more than we would spend at a Denny's. The rain stopped, the day became beautiful, and we spent the morning at the British Museum, and the afternoon at the Imperial War Museum, a sop to Bob who says he likes to "look at big guns" to "see who has the biggest cannon". Must be some testosterone thing. Helena enjoyed the full size walk through replica of a World War I trench, although she complained it was not air conditioned.

I need to emphasize that the passage between sites is lubricated with alcohol, Helena being well hooked on cider again, Bob doing his best to sample every beverage brewed in the UK, and George gazing longingly at anything that drips from the tap. Late that afternoon, we went for a stroll along the Thames to Blackfriars, where we ate supper and drank extensively at the Black Friar, rated one of the ten best pubs in England and site of the very spot where Henry VIII told the pope's envoy to go f*ck himself, that Henry was starting his own church so he could boink Anne Boleyn. When we left, we turned around to take a picture, and a ratty gentleman who saw this weaved toward us. Helena said he was going to ask for money, but instead walked up to Bob and said, "Could you zip me up, mate? I'm f-ing drunk." Bob was taken aback, but the man only meant his jacket, thus ruining a perfect Kodak moment.

We decided to take in a great activity then, perfect for us - a pub crawl with a guide. So for the next two hours, we were led by a professional to the very same pubs we amateurs had visited only hours before. But, a pint's a pint, so Bob and Helena had no problems downing several more.

Tuesday morning we decided to go to the Tower of London, where Bob the history teacher got overexcited. In the Bloody Tower, he decided to leave his mark by splitting his finger open and bleeding on the spot where Richard III killed his two nephews. Later visitors were heard to remark on the realism of the scenery in that room. We also did Westminster Abbey today, and on the way back decided that the meaning of life is now "I drink, therefore I am." George is now done with antibiotics, so the UK better buckle up, as the lion is loose. Tonight we go on a Jack the Ripper after dark walk, and will of course end up "in the pub where Jack's victims may have downed their last pint." Any excuse will do.

Part 3

It's Thursday evening and we have now left London after five tumultuous days. The first thing to report is that we made it on the left hand side of the road. Honestly, there has not been a single problem so far except that every time George screams at Helena to tell him where to turn, Bob starts wheezing like an asthmatic rhino in the back seat. I think he no longer knows how to handle pressure. Screaming at each other is our usual mode of communication, so he better get used to it.

We are currently hitting all the pubs in the little town of Amesbury, about 90 miles SW of London. We are two miles from Stonehenge, which we visited before we came into town.

To pick up where I left off on the London sojourn in Part 2, we had decided to take a night walk visiting the site of every one of Jack the Ripper's murders. It was fascinating, especially visiting all the pubs his hooker victims had patronized. We learned that 40% of all London women at that time were prostitutes, and Bob lamented that he was always too late for the good times.

Helena claimed that her bed was infested with bedbugs that night. Since we had already spent three nights in that room, George suspected that the DTs have begun already for the poor lass.

The next morning we got in the ticket line at Leicester Square and scored front row seats for the sensation of London, the revival of *Guys and Dolls,* and paid only £12.50 per seat, basically what it would cost to see the annual production of *Grease* at Maple Heights High School, former employer of both Bob and George. *Guys and Dolls* was a fantastic production which featured the naked ta-tas of the chorus girls, which made Bob appreciate the play much more, but Helena, as usual, actually became part of the show. First, and remember we are sitting in the front row looking at the orchestra, she started to wink and flirt with a trumpet player, who flirted back and missed a cue for a song. Then at the end of the play the lead female throws a wedding bouquet into the audience. Helena leaps for it, and damned near falls on top of the conductor. She got it, though, and proudly marched through Piccadilly Circus waving it on the way back.

That night we went on a Ghost Walk, and Bob decided to have two pints of ale right before the walk, and forgot to go to the loo. Halfway through the walk he decided he really, really had to pee, and he just disappeared from the tour. This was at 10 o'clock in pitch darkness in a London in which he has never been, so needless to say, he got lost.

After a while, George and Helena decided he wasn't coming back, so they split the free Guinness Bob was supposed to get and went back to the hotel. Bob, meanwhile, had visited every pub for miles squeezing his willie until somebody took pity on him. After excreting a hogshead of liquid, he too decided to go back to the hotel, stopping only three times for another pint. Helena and George arrived hours earlier and had the entire hotel staff out scouring the alleys for him. Nice guy. He says he's sorry but has a devilish grin when he says it.

So that brings us up to today. We took a boat trip to Greenwich to set our watches correctly for once in our lives. 80 degrees and we are all beet red. But when Mr. Strongbow and Mr. Guinness are calling, they cannot be denied, so I have to sign off for now.

Part 4

It has been three or four days since the last posting, but we have been traveling so much we have had no time to look for an internet café. Did I mention that we are driving a Mercedes Benz? They upgraded us because George called the rental agency staff "bloody idiots" and went for their throats when they asked if he wanted a stick shift.

We are writing this from Stratford-upon-Avon. Bob continues his quest to drink England dry, and Helena has joined him pubcrawling as George writes in this internet café. Since we took a Park and Ride bus into town, there is no problem with getting wobbly. Poor George is the designated driver, so they have to be nice to him.

Back in Amesbury, the last place I wrote from, Helena and Bob began a mission to eat every single lamb in the UK. Bob has eaten lamb's liver, a la Hannibal Lecter, and Helena has had lamb loin, lamb shanks, and, I swear to god, lamb's knuckle. There must be a small lamb named Stumpy somewhere near here. George did not sleep in Amesbury because there was a tree full of jackdaws cawing not ten feet away from the window.

The day after Amesbury, we drove to Barnstaple, there conversing with a fishmonger in an open air market who wants to come to America. Bob, already a bit soused by noon, told him he could come to the Hotel Geiser. We then drove to Clovelly, a seaside village which required a one mile hike down steep cobblestone paths at about a 30 degree angle just to visit the place. We paid a man in a Land Rover to drive us back up as none of us could breathe. That night we stayed in Bude, a wonderful seaside town almost empty because it's off-season. There were still many surfers in 54 degree water. There was big excitement as a man caught a nine foot shark four miles offshore.

The next day we drove to Tintagel, the legendary birthplace of King Arthur. Helena decided to get a picture from a cliff which was clearly marked with a sign from the local health office: "Get your dumb arse off this ledge." She stepped on yellow lichen and slipped, being inches from toppling 200 feet into the Atlantic Ocean. George grabbed her, Bob grabbed George's elastic belt, and the Beldens bungeed over the very rocks that Arthur had played on as a lad.

Helena was banned from cider for the rest of the day, but then we felt bad and bought her a bag of Cornish pasties, which she dearly loves. She was heard to exclaim, between bites that she would "rather eat than shit"! That has now become the mantra of this trip.

From Tintagel we went to several lovely Cotswolds thatched roof areas, then decided to find a room. The hostelers remembered the fat Americans from the last trip and had spread the word, because we were turned away from place after place, in Broadway, Chipping Campden, Evesham, Worcester, and even at a wretched place called the Railway Inn which catered to hobos. Wankers apparently did not like Bob's American accent. Eventually, about 7 PM, we found a place in Droitwich - a Holiday Inn Express!

We drove the next morning into Wales, following the line of a canal as it passed over several aqueducts, one a lovely stone arch in Chirk, which then led us to a magnificent castle. Helena became catatonic because she believed George was driving on a footpath, but once committed there was nowhere to turn around, and three miles later it was proven to indeed be a two way road, just a tad narrower than she was used to. We had to wave a Cadbury chocolate under her nose to revive her.

From there we drove to Llangollen, our favorite Welsh town, which has the world's tallest aqueduct, 300 feet above a valley. Imagine a four foot wide cast iron trough of water towering high in the air, with a boat coasting along and a two foot walkway with a small railing along that. Bob took one look at that and damn near fainted. His weak spot has at last been detected. George walked halfway out, met a canal boat, and walked back chatting with the captain, who several times warned him not to take another step without looking as he was about to walk off the edge of the aqueduct and fall on the soccer pitch far below.

From Wales we came back to England, to Chester , and walked the Roman walls around that city. Thence to a drive through the Peaks district, definitely the most difficult driving terrain in the UK, filled with hairpin curves that demand 10 MPH driving. God bless German engineering in automobiles. We ended up in Helena's favorite English town, Bakewell, and stayed in the exact same pub room as on our last trip. In the morning, we found out it was market day and went to a genuine English market filled with farm goods and much merchandise. Bob bought a sweater, George a golf vest, Helena some shampoo because her hair has begun looking like a waif from Dickens, and we loaded up on pastries to tide us over during the day.

Bob has decided that Bakewell, on the River Wye, is where he wants to go when he dies. He loves it as much as Helena does, but he actually checked some real estate prices. The cheapest place listed at £267,000, or about $550,000.

Today is our first real soaking rain, but we are walking about in Stratford anyway. Plans are for Cambridge tomorrow, and Hastings and Brighton Wednesday before returning the car. We may be in Scotland on the bus the next time we get a chance to find a café. The siren call of the pub beckons Bob and Helena once more before we go back to Park and Ride. Cheerio!

Part 5

Hi! We are sitting in Gatwick Airport at 8 PM, waiting for our 6:30 am flight to Glasgow. Yes, we are sleeping here on benches tonight.

The last time we checked in was from Stratford on Avon. We stopped into a pub where Bob and I played our new favorite game, what kind of condom machine will the pub have. The best ones so far have offered whiskey and lager flavored ones, but we have found the most unusual one in the world. This is the honest to god truth: we found a pub with a machine which dispensed, for five pounds, an inflatable vinyl sheep. We did not have five coins in our pocket or we would have brought the evidence home.

We drove to the town of Shirley because we heard there was a launderette. We spent several hours doing laundry, and enduring the locals guffawing at the "huge knickers." Helena says they meant George's, while George is quite sure the opposite was true.

By this time it was almost 6:30, late for finding a room, and sure enough we started the "no room at the inn" routine, but a nice full-up Travelodge found us accommodations in Lutterworth at the Greyhound Inn. Bob "GPS" Geiser decided to take us though back alleys traversed by no human being and only a few donkeys, but we found the pub/hotel finally, although George almost got his first night driving experience.

From there we headed to Cambridge, to ride the double decker and see that university town, which impressed Geiser, who went to Grove City College and thus had never been to a real institute of higher learning before. It was raining for the past few days, but it cleared up enough that the double decker was fine. Two old ladies had the front seats, and when they went off the bus to the loo at a stop, we took their seats and endured their mutterings and druid incantations for the rest of the tour.

We found out the local meaning of the phrase "pub crawl"; in Cambridge it is an annual event involving drinking 17 pints of beer in 19 minutes. Bob bragged that he could do that without even breathing, and we both believe him. He is now down to about 30 minutes of travel before he complains how thirsty he is. "A man might die traveling with you two....have ye no mercy?" he is often heard to exclaim.

Helena and Bob have now eaten lamb nearly every night. Right before I wrote this they both ordered lamb shoulder, then cracked the scapula and sucked the marrow. Both declared the rotator cuff too chewy for their taste.

Last night we were in the town of Battle, where the Battle of Hastings was fought in 1066. Got a great hotel room at the George Hotel. 'Tis a wonderful town with beauteous barmaids. We toured the battlefield this morning behind a group of French students. We joked that 1066 was the last time France won a battle in a war, and then realized that all of them were bilingual and they gave us nasty looks under their unibrowed eyes, so we had to lag behind the rest of the time.

From Battle we discovered a great town, Lewes, which is home to one of England's biggest breweries. Bob thought he was in paradise. We bought sandwiches and ate at the store's outside tables, but George also got a pastie from another shop, and a dishwasher came out and bellowed that eating off-premise food was not permitted and that George must leave immediately. George sheepishly complied, and even dubbed the lad Shitehead to show his appreciation for the reminder.

From there we went to Brighton Beach, the famous English resort. The beach looked like it came from a gravel company. Beach loungers got up with huge pits and welts in their flesh. This did not look like fun. We strolled the pavilion and walkway for awhile before Bob started claiming that the salt water (300 yards away) was making him thirsty, so we hit the pubs and got out of town.

We found a lovely restaurant 10 miles from Gatwick, ate several more British animals, and then drove to return the car, so here we are in an airport, with nothing but time on our hands. They are closing the shops around us, Bob is moaning about thirst, Helena is frantically searching for Cadbury Chocolate to use as a pillow, and I, well, I am the lone sane one still able to type. Hope to write again from Scotland.

Part 6

Hello! The last time we checked in, we were in Gatwick airport. Helena immediately fell asleep on a bench and began snoring loudly enough that Bob and George could not even entertain a thought of sleeping. Neither could anyone else in the airport, as she challenged the local noise ordinances. She ended up sleeping six hours, while George and Bob were doomed to spend 48 hours without sleep. To make it worse, when we got to our Glasgow hotel, George and Helena had the only room not ready, so George ended up sleeping half the night in their lobby, which did not go over very well with the staff, though they dare not bother the very large and very angry looking American. The room turned out to be as hot as a sauna, and had locked windows, so we spent our first night sweating like pigs (er, gammon here in the UK).

Glasgow turned out to be a true armpit of a town, comparable to Pittsburgh at its worst, although we did not see anyone with knuckles scraping the ground like a Steeler fan. Our bus driver/tour guide, Bobby, is really good but incomprehensible. He needs a cigarette often, so we have many loo breaks when on the road. All of our fellow travelers are American except one Irish couple. One 80 year old man loves his pints as much as Geiser. There is also a woman who is so annoying (late for the bus, heavy breathing, general dankness) that we have a pool with three young Californians which will go to the one who kills her.

After Glasgow we headed to the Lochs. First to Loch Lomond, where the driver sang the first of two dozens renditions we have heard of the famous High Road/Low Road song. None of us cares anymore what road they take to Scotland, only that they drive off a cliff and quit singing that damned song.

One of the small towns we went through was Cawdor, which fans of Shakespeare will recognize as the very place of which MacBeth was thane and ruler.

We then went to Loch Ness, where Helena thought she saw the famous monster. Geiser then pointed out that it was really the shadow of the annoying woman standing on the bow of the boat imitating Leo DiCaprio in *Titanic*. We hoped the monster might rise up and eat her, but no such luck.

We then endured a bus ride from Loch Ness over roads that resembled a 10 foot wide West Virginia Turnpike. George keeps falling asleep and Geiser seems to take perverse delight in pointing out sights in a loud voice and seeing George jump. Geiser has not slept on this entire trip. He is like a drunken Energizer bunny.

That night we stayed at the best hotel we have ever seen in the UK, in the town of Nairn. There is a famous beach and golf course right down the road. Helena wanted to "kill two birds with one stone" by walking the town and beach at dusk. It was Friday night trollop night (a UK tradition) and all the hoors were out on the street. This disoriented Geiser's legendary and self-proclaimed but little seen GSP system (FUBAR, for those who know the meaning of that acronym), and he proceeded to lead us assuredly on the road back to Loch Lomond. 10 miles and many hours later, we found our way back so that we were able to get a couple hours sleep in the magnificent hotel room. Thanks, Geiser.

Yesterday we hit the road again. The annoying woman forgot her passport and money at the hotel, so we had to do a U turn back. As a busload, we voted to pull away and leave her, but the bussie has a conscience and doesn't get paid for dead passengers, so we had to wait.

We next went to a castle owned by a lord whose coat of arms is two naked men with manacles on. The last three earls died childless for assorted reasons. Then we went to a distillery. The name of the whiskey they produce is Blair Atholl. We drank several free shots and got toasted and spent the next few hours calling each other "you atholl." One has to say it fast to get the point.

We arrived in Edinburgh last night. Geiser fell in love with the town. The castle in the middle is built on top of an extinct volcano and rises up in the city center on a tower of basalt. It's quite a sight. We went to a dinner and show of traditional Scottish song, dance, and jokes. It was pretty entertaining, with only one rendition of "Loch Lomond," but the final song was a singalong to the Robert Burns song that everybody knows, "Alde Lang Syne." We had to join hands with our neighbor and sing lustily. One guess who was sitting next to Bob, panting like a St. Bernard in heat. Yep, the exceedingly moist woman. Bob refused to hold her hand, so she barked "Goddamn it, he said to hold hands and you're going to hold mine." Geiser was so intimidated he actually did it. This was after he had eaten two full plates of *haggis*, the repulsive sausage made from the parts of the cow even hyenas won't eat, so I have now witnessed Geiser behaving in ways I could not have believed possible.

We have a great hotel room which has a full view of the castle out the window. We did a city tour this morning, and afterward witnessed another cataclysmic event. Geiser has become a soccer fan. Geiser, the legendary hater who was allegedly a drum major at Eastlake North High School, now loves footie. Yesterday was the Scottish professional championship, and an Edinburgh team won the title. Just two hours ago, 400,000 Edinburgers and three Yanks stood on the street cheering hysterically as the team rode by on a double decker waving the Scottish Cup. Geiser even learned the chants: "Hearts (Of Midlothian, the name of the team) are having a party" and "Hybies (the Hybernians, archenemies of the Hearts) are gay." Bob has become a soccer hooligan. I feel a chill in Hades!

Tonight we will go on a pub crawl, the first since London, visiting all the Edinburgh literary high points. Bob is gritting his teeth, but the soccer buzz he got earlier, along with several pints of Abbott's Ale, will keep him in good spirits. See you from Ireland...................

Part 7

Hello from Ireland! We have been three days on the Emerald Isle, with two more until we return home. The last thing we did in Scotland was a literary pub crawl. George loved it, but Helena and Bob decided that they would gouge out their own eyes before they ever did that again. Peasants. We also were running out of money so we had to economize on the pub part, and the guide thought we were very strange, taking turns drinking from a half pint of ale.

The flight to Dublin was fine, and about half of the people from our Scotland tour are on the Irish tour too. For those who remember our last trip to Ireland, I have been counting, and "Danny Boy" has been sung only once. The trip's not over, but it appears I will not have to tear my ears off.

We had a tour of Dublin the first day, and that evening went to an Irish cabaret. It consisted of Irish dancing, which resembles zombies bouncing really fast with broken arms, and an 80 year old comedian who thought that using "Murphy" and "O'Malley" in the same sentence would produced gales of laughter. It did, in fact, as the audience, which averaged about 90 years old, must have known all these people in their youth. We, however, did not get to hear all the punchlines over the growling of our bellies, as we were the very last of 500 people to get served our dinner.

The next morning our bus never arrived at the hotel, having worn out its starter, so we had to wait two hours for a replacement. Bob used the free time to look for a statue of Molly Malone, the cockles and mussels tart of legend. We saw the statue on the way in, and she had a low bodice, which got him excited, and he wanted to take a picture. Once our new bus came in, we set off for Killarney (the company did buy us a free drink that evening, so one can hardly hate them. Bob wanted to sabotage the bus again the next morning to see if we could get two pints the next time).

We went to an Irish farmhouse for scones and tea. Picture Geiser sitting down to scones and tea. I tell you, he is becoming so European. First a love of soccer, and now high tea. Next up was Blarney Castle, where Bob and Helena kissed the Blarney Stone. George was banned from the experience as he had set off an HIV alert six years earlier by bleeding on the stone, and his picture was still being circulated by Interpol. Bob did not enjoy being 150 feet in the air, upside down, kissing a rock, but since he hasn't kissed anything in such a long time, he still got stimulated by the experience. Helena ate Irish stew at a pub, this being the 12th different way that she has ravaged a little lamb on this trip.

Today was a horrid day, a soaking rain, and this was the day to drive the Ring of Kerry. This trip makes the West Virginia turnpike look like the Autobahn. We do have an unbelievable driver, and he navigated the 10 foot wide road clinging precariously to the side of mountains with ease. The rain finally let up, and all of us agree that we got to see scenery unrivaled on the face of the earth. Tonight we are on our own, which generally means getting fully blotto, although the European soccer championship is on TV tonight, and Bob is getting very excited about watching it and wants to be done with supper so he can see it all, including the pre-game. He is out buying a Arsenal jersey to wear. Folks, he is not the same man.

Part 8

We are back in the states, and it is time to draw an end to this honest truth of everything that happened on our momentous trip to UK. First of all, Helena wants everyone to know that she did not gain a single pound on the trip. I asked her if she meant weight, or the innumerable pounds she spent on chocolate, and she got mad at me, for some reason. It must be because Monday was her birthday, and she is now a very old lady once again, at least until October, when I reach her Methuselah-like age.

We last left off with Geiser preparing to watch his first ever soccer game in Killarney. We sat in the pub of our hotel and watched it on large screen, and, primed with a few pints of Old Speckled Hen Ale, Geiser immediately got into the action. With lusty shouts of "drive the lane" and "take it to the hole," he attracted the attention of everyone in the room, who realized that he was using basketball terms to describe an interminably slow foot-oriented sport. The Arsenal goalkeeper got kicked out 18 minutes into the game, and, judging by Geiser's groans, you would have thought we were watching reruns of Ernest Byner's fumble that doomed the 1987 Cleveland Browns. Eventually, Barcelona wore down the short-handed Gunners, and Geiser was heart-broken. He asked if this summer's World Cup would be on US television, as he is now as fully hooked as a big-mouthed bass on one of our buddy Tim's beloved fishing shows.

The next day we finished our tour of Ireland with a visit to the Cliffs of Mohr, reputedly the windiest spot in the northern Hemisphere. Four Germans were sucked over the cliffs last year, which did little to make us want to get up close and personal. Geiser kept whining that his "skinny little butt will get blown over" and Helena wanted to duplicate her Evel Knievel escapades on the yellow lichen at Tintagel, but George remained clear headed (and exhausted from the climb to the top of the cliffs) so both Geiser and Helena stayed close in case he needed CPR.

That night we went to Bunratty Castle for a medieval feast, eaten entirely with the fingers and a dagger. They did not use forks because they knew George would stick one in his eye if they sang "Danny Boy" – which they in fact did. George thus had to be prevented from ocular self-mutilation. The highlight of the evening was an 18 month old baby who was left to wander around and walked on stage with the purpose of joining the Celtic harpist in her solo. Denied the opportunity with a swift kick from the musician, the child began screaming, and the mortified mother grabbed her and ran with her into the only non-occupied room: the castle's dungeon. We loved watching the little shit behind bars for the rest of the evening. Mead, the alcoholic drink made from fermented honey, was passed around, and Geiser was heard asking his female neighbors if he could lick their cups, thus enhancing our Ugly American image.

The next morning we departed from the Shannon airport for the USA. The Munster Rugby team, from Ireland, was departing from the airport to go to Cardiff to play Biarritz for the European championship, and they were walking through when Helena was returning from the loo. Oblivious as usual (she was jingling the last of her euro coins, thinking about the final Cadbury's chocolate bars they would buy), and just by coincidence dressed in the Munster team colors, she joined the team as it walked the concourse to the applause of every Irishman in the airport. She beamed with pride, thinking they were happy she had contributed so much to their economy via her appetite for lamb, cider, and chocolate, but in fact Geiser and George heard someone comment about the ancient groupie who had latched on to these NFL-sized athletes. Helena's new nickname is now Groupie Granny, and she was whispered about all the way across the Atlantic.

We were in the next to the last row of the airplane, and we thought the last row was empty, until right before they closed the door, who should come down the aisle but the Dungeon Baby from the night before. Fortunately, her parents had apparently saved some mead for her bottle, because she was unconscious for the whole flight.

But across the aisle from Geiser was one of the biggest jerks in the world, a drunken Irishman who quaffed six bottles of wine on the trip. Drunk out of his mind, he first tried to get some French Canadians to teach him how to say "fu*k" in French. After they ignored him, he then tried to get them to answer some riddles. Since they did not speak English, this also stymied him. Giving up on them, he tried to pick up a chunky elementary teacher in the next row by doing stupid coin tricks.

All of this was approximately two feet from Geiser, and if you know him, you know his impersonation of Mount Vesuvius when he's getting pissed off. But being an administrator has taught him patience, what with having to deal with those gum chewers they toss out of class at Willoughby South High School, so he did not have to be arrested when we landed.

Helena is adding up the total cost of the trip, and it looks like her first year of pension has now been blown on chocolate and cider, so I guess it was a success after all.

The Beldens Go To Europe, 2008

Having survived innumerable trips to Myrtle Beach and Hilton Head for golf, wherein Bob Geiser and George played 36 holes of golf every single day and then treated Helena like a princess for two hours before falling asleep, usually over meals at a restaurant, with a bottle of beer hovering nearby, and then rose in the darkness to do it again for seven consecutive days;

And having survived the legendary tour of England, Ireland, Wales and Scotland in 2006, which resulted in an acute shortage of chocolate, cider and mutton in the United Kingdom, as Helena and Geiser, after daily inhaling several pints of ale and cackling fiendishly,, ate damned near every lamb on the island, while George issued drunken political diatribes which are commonly acknowledged to have caused the fall of the Labour government of Tony Blair;

And having survived a 4000 mile trip to Texas to watch 20 minutes of six-man football in the metropolis of Richland Springs Texas, population 126; getting back to San Antonio at 1 AM and playing golf the next morning at the Pecan Valley course on which Julius Boros won the 1968 United States Open (though George doubted Julius had to tee off at 5:45 AM and play the first three holes in complete darkness, thus losing 5 balls per hole), and then driving to Austin, aka "The San Francisco of Texas", where Geiser, after a lengthy stop to drain a tavern dry, was caught ogling an obvious transvestite and exclaiming "Wow, do they have some nice women here!" (to which George , after eyeballing the person who had so delighted Geiser's vision, replied acidly, "Have you ever heard of .... KONG?");

They now proposed to leave on Wednesday May 21 for a flight to Venice, where they will spend a couple days, then board a cruise ship ominously nicknamed the TITANIC II , to visit unsuspecting ports in Greece, Croatia, Italy, France, and Spain, with a couple days in Barcelona at the end.

George doesn't know the exact itinerary, as Helena and Geiser, for the last six months, had weekly breakfast covens where they huddled and talked in code about various ports of call and how much they plan to spend (thank goodness for the Ohio STRS pension fund and the automatic 3% cost of living increase, because this one could bankrupt the trio, what with the enfeebled dollar). At these conspiratorial meals, George was told to mind his own business and just eat , that he will be told where they are on a need-to-know basis and not before. All he knows is that his befuddlement will last something over two weeks.

But George is devious, and has purchased an Asus EEE mini-laptop with built in WiFi, no bigger than a paperback novel, on which he will hunt and peck the trip as it happens, as usual without embellishment or exaggeration of any sort, as he hides in the tiny quarters he shares with Helena, trying to escape the horrors of the bloody Mediterranean sun while Geiser trolls for ancient crones (as he says, "I'd prefer that they be breathing, but whatever..."), and Helena waits hours for the "free complimentary drink" they claim has alcohol in it, eyes the cabin boys, and dreams of what might have been.

Part 2

This might not look like any language with which the reader is familiar, since George has discovered that his fat rolls prevent the tiny laptop from sitting flat on his lap, but the trip has begun, and they are at the airport.

During the drive to the airport, Helena regaled the boys with stories about people who got diarrhea during safety drills on the ship, probably preparing them for any accidents she might have. The TSA goons decided that a flotilla of senior citizens in wheelchairs looked like terrorists, so it took quite a while to get through security while they wanded them and their wheelchairs kept setting off alarms. The trio feel so much safer now. Anyway, they have two hours until they get stuffed into a plane for Philadelphia and thence to Venice.

The hop to Philadelphia wasn't bad, except the guy behind them must have been the regional manager for a salami factory, as he thickened the air in the entire airplane. Customs was a breeze, and got they onto the flight to Venice quickly. The man in front of Helena immediately flopped his seat back, putting his bald head in her lap for the entire nine hour flight. It didn't bother her as she also fell into a coma for the whole trip.

Geiser even fell asleep, until he woke up to a sexy Katherine Heigl movie, *27 Dresses*, and his eyes almost popped out of his head and he moaned loudly, not realizing how he was entertaining the plane since he had headphones on and couldn't hear himself. George slept not a wink, feeling like someone had injected a liter of Novocaine into his ass. It was so numb he had to be extra vigilant not to commit a social error.

Helena woke up looking like Keith Richards of the Rolling Stones and badly in need of Visine, with red eyes that looked like the undead in a George Romero movie. She tried to go to the lav without her glasses and crashed into the flight attendant's food cart. She also scared a young girl who thought she was a zombie, but George told Helena to put on her sunglasses and she didn't freak out anyone else.

They arrived in Venice, a city with a terrible infrastructure. It must have rained a lot lately because all the roads are under water and one has to take a boat to get through the streets. They took a water taxi called the *vaporetto* (which Bob think means little farter) to Piazza San Marco, where they had their first run-in with the police. Having bought a sandwich and Coke (beer for Bob) they sat on a bench in San Marco to eat it, when a squad of Keystone Kops yelled at them (rudely speaking in Italian, not English) to get out of the square. There are a million pigeons who descend on food and peck out the eyes of people who eat in the plaza. Knowing they couldn't get back to the hotel without eyes, they grudgingly complied.

The Coke in a 12 ounce bottle was $7, by the way.

At their hotel, which overlooks the Grand Canal, George tried to clean up and complained that he had to get on his knees to use the sink. Helena explained it was a bidet and it is not his face he should wash in it. These Italians have some strange customs.

Helena discovered the wonder of gelato, Italian ice cream, and now no longer complains that the boys didn't buy her a plank of chocolate for her birthday. She fell in love with the gelato huckster when he told her he had hazelnut flavor. She threw up her hands and almost fell backward into the Grand Canal. Since their hotel overlooked the canal, they left their windows open when they went to sleep. At 3 AM they discovered that, unlike England, Italy has mosquitoes, and sleep was hard to come by between slaps the rest of the night..

Friday was check-in day on the ship. Helena had done her research and determined that they needed to take Bus 6 on line A3 from Piazzo Roma. She neglected to note what company owned which bus 6, so they confidently boarded a bus for the five minute ride to the ship, only to discover that THIS unairconditioned bus 6 went to MARGHERA, a town 50 kilometers away. It might be in Portugal, as that was the language of all their fellow passengers. Two hours later they were deposited on exactly the same square meter from which they had departed, so they ended up walking the mile to their ship hauling two suitcases apiece, uphill all the way. Even svelte Geiser was sweating like a slaughterhouse pig. It took much alcohol to get him back to normal. Helena wants to go back to town tonight to meet the gelato gigolo, but she goes alone.

Part 3

It was Saturday, although already months and days have little connection to the travelers' reality. Yesterday they decided to leave the ship and take the *vaporetto* to the island of Murano. Their cruise line was no longer running shuttles into town, and they have become quite adept at looking like generic tourists and joining ANY shuttle bus queue. Helena chats up the people in line and they just kind of ooze along with everyone else into any available seat.

Murano was a very nice artisan town devoted to the art of glass making. The Murines, which must be what they call themselves, hate the Chinese, since every window had a nasty sign belittling the quality of Chinese glass and saying it was destroying their economy. An Asian couple walking ahead of them kept throwing furtive looks over their shoulders, as if the Beldens would rat them out and claim they were artglass bootleggers or something. Bob bought a very nice heart-shaped vase to put on his mantel, to prove to anyone who knows him that he does indeed have a heart and can now actually show them.

This morning Helena, being in love with this fascinating city, decided she wanted one more traipse through the maze of Venice streets and canals. Bob and George complied, though George's feet were not really much in accord with the plans. He did not complain as he knows the utter futility of that, once Helena is locked and loaded on a mission.

Back on ship, they had their mandatory lifeboat drill. George got to stand next to the obligatory as*hole for this cruise, who complained loudly when they repeated the instructions in both English and Italian, quipping that if they couldn't speak English they didn't deserve to live. A woman close by chose that moment to faint, precluding George from smacking the as*hole on the back of his head with the 500 page book he was carrying to read while hiding from the sun.

As they were leaving port, Helena stood topside to wave like they used to in World War II newsreels. Bob is already part of the Speedo squadron in the hot tub, and when they wake up they should be in Dubrovnik, Croatia.

They met their tablemates tonight – two Texas oilmen and their wives. After four courses, they discovered that one wife is a school secretary, and the other is a former school principal who now is a university professor, so at least they had a lot in common with them. By the time dessert was done, they discovered that all four dislike President George Bush as much as the Beldens do, so it should be a good two weeks.

That is, if they can stay out of the onboard bars. They tried two tonight, and found a singer who looked like televangelist Ernest Angley crooning "I Left My Heart in San Francisco," which made them run laughing into another bar, where they found Moms Mabley in a Red Hat Club outfit butchering Cole Porter. Another hasty retreat brought Bob into contact with a Dick Cheney lookalike headed to late supper, and he did not appreciate any impediment to that path. They did find a fellow passenger who is an absolute clone of George's sister Rosemary, right down to bobbing her head while Ernest Angley sang Del Shannon's song "Runaway."

Lest the reader think them randy devils, though, they have been in bed by nine every night of the trip.

The next day, they took a ferry into the port of Dubrovnik, a gorgeous enclave on the Dalmatian Coast of the Adriatic Sea. It is the furthest south city in Croatia, squooshed right up next to Montenegro. The mountains come right down to the shore, leaving just enough level space to build the houses which climb the mountainside. It reminded Helena and George of the town of Avalon on Catalina Island. The water is absolutely clear; they are anchored in the middle of the bay but can see almost to the bottom.

Most Dubrovnik buildings are modern, since every 20 years or so Croatia has a civil war, destroys everything, and has to rebuild. Great for the construction industry, apparently.

They took a bus tour through the countryside and had a meal at a restaurant/trout farm. Two lads came down to a trout pen, dipped in a plastic box, and hauled about 10 thrashing fish up to the restaurant where they were on plates and in the bellies of the trio before they reboarded the bus. Their last stop was the Old Town, surrounded by Great Wall of China type defenses, the best example of a walled city in Europe. Only 1500 people live inside. It has a worse maze of streets than Venice, and reminded them of the Shambles of York England, where one can reach out and touch each side of the street.

Other than a pigeon pooping on George as he listened intently to the tour guide, no nastiness accompanied the trip. They did recognize one bald head; it was the guy whose head was in Helena's lap for nine hours on the flight over. He turned out to be a Louisiana State fan, so George, a Big Ten loyalist, disliked him even more.

Tonight they get a "Broadway revue" starring two aerialists who spin from the ceiling. No one could recall what Broadway show that was from.

Part 4

Today was an at-sea day, and Helena and Bob have joined the should-never-be-seen-in-public masses in swimsuits at the pool for a day of lounging. George visited them and saw a 90 year old, 80 pound woman in a bikini, which sight seared his vision and he vowed not to make the mistake again. They are once again in the youngest 10 percent of the passengers. Bob's prediction of coeds on a graduation cruise was sadly well off-mark.

Besides, George took his first water pill of the trip and was tethered to the bathroom for the next three hours. Bob has not taken one the whole trip, which must account for his increasingly bloated appearance.

George instead decided to attend lectures today. He listened to "The Life of Frank Sinatra" by a guy who once pecked Tina Sinatra on the cheek as his claim to fame. Later that day a Greek professor was going to talk about "The Golden Age of Greece.' After that he will go to the theater where he will watch the beginners class for Broadway Dancing. All the fat guys with no concept of body size and/or sense of public shame will try to hoof it like Gene Kelly. It's usually quite a sight, and people on other decks wonder why a calm sea has suddenly become so turbulent.

Yes, it's a slow day for your writer.

Last night's Broadway Revue was actually very good and professional. They did vignettes from *The Producers* (if one has ever seen the chorus line production number of grannies with their walkers from that show, it's a fair representation of their fellow passengers); *Mamma Mia* (ooh, the flaming boy dancers really got to strut in that one); *The Lion King* (that's where the aerialists came in, and they were really visually spectacular); *Chicago*; *Hairspray*, and *Wicked*. Helena and George had seen all but *Wicked* on Broadway, and Bob had seen *Lion King* in Toronto, so they had a basis of comparison and the cruise kids acquitted themselves well. George still and always will hate *Lion King*, but if they ever do *My Fair Lady* he will be happy.

Tonight the featured performer was an "internationally acclaimed pianist," and since they are off the coast of Albania, if one person clapped, he was entitled to list that in his resume. The Beldens were NOT in attendance.

Tomorrow their shore trip to Santorini Greece begins at 7:15, so it was their usual early bedtime, once more missing the mysterious Gourmet Gobble at midnight.

Part 5

Today was Tuesday, they thought, and they docked at Santorini Greece in the middle of the Aegean Sea. If one is following the intrepid Argonauts, they were 65 miles north of the island of Crete. It was about 75 degrees outside under an azure sky, exactly what one would picture an ideal Mediterranean scene would be.

The southern end of Santorini (St. Theresa) contains the archaeological excavations which are believed to be the legendary Atlantis, but Greece botched their public preparation for the 2004 Olympics and no one has been allowed to visit them for four years. "Maybe this year, or next, or maybe sometime," their guide told them when asked when they would be reopened.

Santorini belongs to an island chain called the Cyclades, because the chain is circular. There is an active volcano right off their port bow which blew out in fairly recent times in geological terms. The volcano sank, the sea rushed in, and the islands are the peaks of the mountain range near the volcano. The water between the islands, this huge circular pool, is the "caldera", or cauldron.

But when Zeus decided to do this, he screwed up the topography by putting the ports at sea level and the towns 1000 feet higher. So when the group took the ferry to shore, they were the lucky ones who had a bus waiting. People who did not sign up for an excursion had three choices: a trek on a zigzag path up a 30 degree slope, or wait in a long line to pay for a cable car tram straight up the slope, OR pay a wiry old coot who would load you onto the back of a weary looking donkey to carry you up the zigzag. One whiff of the donkey told them that they did not want to be anywhere near anyone who chose that method (if one has ever been to a donkey basketball game, there are few odors in nature to rival a ripe ass).

But bus travelers were they, and the first town they went to was the quaint village of Oia, which in Greek is pronounced "yee-haw." Pretty much every building in this town is whitewashed with a blue roof, distinct to the Greek Islands. There is no land here – being volcanic, it's just rocks. Even the paths which comprise its few thoroughfares are pretty much just carved into the island itself. The town was filled with lots of little shops, and their guide assured them there was no way to get lost.

He didn't reckon on the navigational skills of the three, though. It wasn't really their fault – it was the damned dogs. Every home has one, and when the denizens work in the shops, the dogs run loose. They are very tame and friendly, and also the laziest creatures in the world. When tired, they just collapse on the spot. Also, since there is no land, they poop there too. The Beldens weren't very far into the stroll when they started smelling the most godawful stench coming from the people in front of them. Now Geiser and George play with the Monday Morning Golf Buddies and are used to stenches, but Helena was the one who noticed the Crocs on the feet of the lady in front of them were coated with brown gore.

Since the guide told them there was no way to get lost on the way back to the bus, they decided to avoid these canine offerings to the underworld and take the path less traveled. They soon discovered that the village dump of the town of Oia, through which they subsequently voyaged, is where the poop is dumped when the town burghers decide to scrape it up. A double nasal whammy was their reward for courageous exploration, and they just made in back to the bus, wheezing and malodorous.

Their next stop was the world famous Santorini Winery. Helena sampled red (very good but dry), Bob had the white (which he enjoyed lip-smackingly), and George had their trademark Santovino, which he decided tasted like vintage Romilar CF cough medicine, slightly past its sell-by date.

They were then whisked (every 100 feet is a hairpin curve, so whisked is a gross exaggeration) to the actual town of Santorini, which is one of the most picturesque tourist traps one can find. It is so pretty the tourist isn't insulted by how commercial it is. All three agreed that climbing and poop-dodging makes a soul thirsty, so their contribution to the Greek economy was quaffing bottles of *Mythos* lager beer.

Now they had to get DOWN to the dock to catch the ferry. Walk ....or straddle a donkey ... or ride the cable car, a duration of exactly 80 seconds. One look over the precipice and the thin strand of wire holding six cars with six passengers each, and Robert K. Geiser, former Major in the Grove City College Air Force ROTC, ejaculated "There's no f**** way you are getting me on that thing." Helena had to promise to hold his hand, and Bob made George ride in a separate car "to balance the weight" before he would step in. Only once before, in Llangollen Wales on top of a canal aqueduct with a two foot wide walkway over a bottomless gorge, had RKG exhibited this unusual quirk, but this only makes the Beldens love him more.

Less than an hour later they were back on the ship, well fed at the luncheon buffet, and Bob had resumed his usual position blocking the path around the outdoor pool, growing more lobster-like in skin tone. Helena was hiding in the shadows reading a novel about an fat girl whose ex-lover wrote a newspaper article about what loving a fat girl was like, and George was ensconced in the ship library creating this account without any deviation from the facts.

Part 6

The tiny Asus computer was turning out to be a boon. Of course, the tiny keyboard was giving George fits, what with all the mistypings that crop up, but it was so much better than having to find an Internet cafe, and then having to spill out all his musings in a certain time limit. The library, about 50 feet from their room, is a WiFi hotspot, and George had it down to about three minutes to log on, copy and paste and send his writings, read any incoming mail, check Google news for any important world happenings, and log off.

Yesterday they went into Athens, and after much anticipation were vastly underwhelmed. They were docked in the city of Piraeus, contiguous with Athens, which has a population of four million, over 1/3 of the entire Greek population. Mile upon mile of stacked featureless flats, abominable traffic (double parking was the standard here, and triple parking nearly the norm), and interminable ugliness (no slums though). They were crawling along and suddenly, in the middle of this wretched mess they suddenly came upon a world famous structure, and just as suddenly the city swallowed the bus up again. The Parthenon was swaddled in scaffolding, and they got no closer to the Akropolis than half a mile away and downhill from it.

George was thrilled to see the 1896 Olympic stadium, where Pierre de Coubertin resurrected the idea of the Olympics. 69,000 continuous marble bench style seats, a tiny infield and track barely wide enough to contain six lanes of runners, and still looking as if it had been built yesterday. The 2004 Olympic archery contests and the end of the marathon were held here.

They then traveled in 95 degree heat to the Plaxos, the old shopping district, which today has high end and gypsy vendors side by side. They were vastly entertained by the tablecloth ladies, a multitude of old crones selling linen tablecloths, who ceaselessly accosted every passerby with their wares. They knew come-on phrases in every language on earth, and if one didn't respond in one language they kept hectoring in other tongues, hoping to get a response. They offered them at 50 euros, and several shipmates bargained them down to 15.

Apparently license-less, they scattered like rats when the police showed up. George and Helena were royally entertained when Bob downed several *Alta Greek* beers and unsuccessfully tried to hit on their tour guide, Penny. Bob has a cold, so the sound of his phlegmy hacking while coming up with corny seduction lines might have had something to do with her indifference.

They had open seating at dinner last night, so their regular table partners, drawling oilman J. R. Ewing (aka Mark), his wife Lindy, a "quiet talker" for *Seinfeld* fans, and their friends Bill the short and his big haired college professor wife Jeannie, were absent, to be replaced by Dick and Mary from Waukesha Wisconsin, who had each substitute taught a couple days after retirement (any college grad can sub in the Cheesehead public schools). They thought they knew everything that is wrong with modern schools. Dick (a fitting name) told a hilarious story about his first day when he told an entire class of kids that they were irredeemably stupid and would do the world a favor by dying soon. The Beldens' silence did not deter him and his viper-tongued wife, who never stopped talking, thus ensuring that the bulk of her meal fell on her ample bosom. This being "white clothes night" she looked like a Jackson Pollock painting when they finally left. The Beldens will run like hell if they ever see them again.

Later, they had a lamb roast, and Helena and Bob were very excited by the prospect of devouring more of God's innocents, but they thought they could combine their regular dinner (at which Bob ate veal cheeks) with this Bacchanalian repast, and discovered that their belt refused to budge any further, so they actually stuffed themselves rather listlessly. George retired to the fitness room during their excesses to keep his trim and lithe figure attractive. George also got up at 6 AM this morning to power-walk two miles on top of the ship. George is a good boy.

George wrote this segment sitting in the massive Waterfall Cafe, the main feeding trough of the ship. He was sitting in the section the Japanese had commandeered, so he was getting a lot of strange looks, probably because they were fascinated with the computer. There was not a word of English within 10 yards, so there are no intelligible conversations to distract him.

Their ship, the *Celebrity Summit,* is always the largest one in port. It has 12 decks; George once took the elevator to deck one, but was chased away, because that is where a long row of naked men chained to benches sat rowing and being whipped, and the management would prefer passengers to not know about this new mode of "green" locomotive power they have adopted in this ecologically-minded era.

Deck two is guest services where one can purchase overpriced tour excursions, visit the Ecuadoran doctor who has tribal masks and spears over his door, or schedule a trip to the dentist, whose main job seems to be returning missing full dentures to people who drop them in the pool.

Deck 3 has the cinema, where four year old movies are shown on screens the size of computer monitors. Deck 4 and 5 have the Celebrity Theater in the fore of the ship, a Las Vegas style showroom that doubles as the Bingo parlor, definitely the highlight of the day for most passengers. Bingo seems to be the only word common to the 50 or so languages one can hear on the trip.

Also on deck 4 and 5 in the center of the ship is their nightly restaurant. According to the daily dictates of the ship's schedule, they have three modes of dress for dinner, casual, informal (sports jacket) , and formal (tux or dark suit). George dresses exactly the same for every meal, which is whatever clothes don't smell funky, and no one has said a word. Bob is more conscious of public approbation and dresses according to the schedule. On formal night he auditions for his next career, appearing to be a plump mortician. Helena wears whatever currently fits.

Decks 6,7,8,and 9 are mainly staterooms for the plebeians. Truthfully, they had no complaints at all in that regard in their deck 8 coffins. George and Helena had a giant king sized bed which allows them to snore away without waking each other (Helena more than George, as George has never heard himself snore even once). Bob was on the other side of the wall, and if he is sneaking any moaners into his room after hours, they hadn't heard it. The flush system in the bathroom was like the ones on airplanes, where all production was swiftly and loudly whisked away to a central collection point, so it was audibly apparent when a neighbor had finished their morning poop.

Lorna, their room steward, was very nice and visited their room three or four times a day to straighten up and replace towels. Gifted with a incredible gag reflex, she patiently folded every single pair of underwear George had left hanging on the mirror so he could get one more day of usage out of them.

Deck 10 is the pool, whirlpools, and the heated indoor thalassotherapy pool where everybody who is ashamed to show their bodies in public can wallow in a shallow bubbly pond, away from the slit-eyed glare of the few hardbodies on board. This is conveniently located next to the Waterfall Grill where George sits, so the porkers can leave their shame-drenched ablutions and traipse dripping wet in there to grab another tray of cookies or gallon of ice cream to eat before heaving themselves back into the fetid water.

Deck 11 has the track where George so faithfully (once this trip) performed his walking regimen.

Deck 12 is the Titanic deck where people thought they could emulate Leo DiCaprio's "King of the World" routine. The Celebrity people have thoughtfully surrounded the prow with electrified barbed wire to preclude drunken sots from pitching headlong into what is now the Mediterranean Sea. There was a toga party last night, featuring many fabrics purchased from the Athens tablecloth ladies, and some would-be Belushis would have happily and obliviously toppled over the starboard side while being well in their cups.

Scattered at convenient places on nearly every deck are cabarets, bars, lounges, and cigar boutiques eager to hydrate passengers with liquids of varied and sundry abilities to render one completely insensate. The Beldens had visited them all, and the Ernest Angley clone had the remarkable power of appearing instantly, crooning a mangled ballad whenever they settled in.

So that was their ship. Tonight they have advertised a British Invasion trivia contest in the Rendezvous Lounge, so George would challenge whatever gray matter he hasn't pickled to recall whether it was Freddie and the Dreamers or Gerry and the Pacemakers who did "Ferry Cross The Mersey."

Part 7

Thursday night was British Invasion trivia night, so despite the fact that they had to get up at 5:30 the next morning to spend 10 hours in Pompeii and Naples, the intrepid trio fortified themselves with dinner (George having finally refused to bear the yoke of formal night and eating instead with the peasants in the Waterfall Cafe while Helena and Bob dined on filet mignon and lamb, respectively) and several rounds of drinks. They marched to the Revelation Lounge at 9:30, an hour early. There they found a live Hispanic band which specialized in 60's music. They were, in fact, the Mexican Beatles, so dubbed by Bob, which immediately transmogrified into *Los Cucarachos Mejicanos*, a close approximation meaning the Mexican Cockroaches. The lead singer was a senorita with whom Bob, several Absoluts to the wind, fell madly in love. If her brother, a Pancho Villa surrogate who sang falsetto in songs requiring such a harmony, had not been so menacing, Bob might have received, to quote Mick Jagger, some "Satisfaction," which song they had indeed butchered during the evening.

Then the Trivia contest began, a name that tune and performer test of twenty selections only a few bars long apiece. George began to worry because several of the teams were Limeys who gasped and started scratching their answer sheets after a single note. After several early missteps, including being unable to place a female singer, and Bob insisting that "Sunshine of Your Love" by Cream was "In A Gadda Da Vida", George got on a roll and confidently nailed the last 17 selections, song and singer.

The host began the grading process, on the honor system. The female singer turned out to be Cilla Black, and the version of "Apache" they played was by the Shadows, not Jorgen Ingmann, who had the American hit version.

And then the real excitement began. Four of the selections, by The Turtles, The Byrds, The Box Tops, and the Left Banke, were not by British artists, and despite getting the answers, George loudly bellowed each time that the artists were not English, and the poor frustrated host was not pleased at being heckled. After the fourth time, he mused aloud into the mike that perhaps they should call security. But when the answers were tallied, Our Gang had 37 of 40 right to take top prize, and they each won a Celebrity Cruises visor which none of them will ever wear.

George's obnoxiousness was ameliorated when he went to the host and congratulated him on his grace and bearing in being revealed as an ignoramus, thus earning a reprieve from being made to walk the gangplank. Murmurs of "industry insider" ran through the crowd, but the Brits recognized greatness and congratulated one whom they recognized as their superior. The host even asked for their room number, and they expected a horse's head under their sheets when they returned this evening.

George's reward was a night spent completely without sleep due to aching feet from forgetting, in his moment of triumph, to take pain pills and having cramping feet all night from his two mile walk that morning, a mistake he will not soon repeat.

Part 8

This installment was so tardy because, since Friday at 7 AM, they had been on the ship only to sleep and catch a few 5000 calorie meals to sustain them. Helena, in her delusion that they are still the 18 year old kids who could do EVERYTHING like bunnies (yep, that's what he means), had scheduled them for four consecutive tour excursions that averaged 11 hours on shore.

Yesterday, Friday, they docked in Naples for their trip innocently tagged "Amalfi Drive and Pompei." They figured they'd see a couple Italian villas, a couple incinerated hovels, and be back on the ship in no time.

Silly Americans. Amalfi drive was 51 kilometers of 15 kph twists and turns clinging to the tops of the mountain range of which Mount Vesuvius is merely the beginning. It begins in Naples, and wends its way down to Salerno, passing through the legendary towns of Sorrento, Positano, Praiano, and Amalfi. Seeing Vesuvius was a real treat, but the constant back and forth of hairpin turns in an unending procession of buses, scooters, cars, and motorcycles, plus the occasional bicyclist and witless wandering hikers, took a toll on one's ability to process beauty.

The best part was when they drove by Sophia Loren's five story villa clinging to a hillside over the Gulf of Salerno. Their tour guide looked out the window and said, "Hey, Sophia, put some clothes on!" Five Japanese men immediately leaped across the bus and smashed their heads on the windows trying to look. Bob and George sat and calculated that she is 77 years old and even if she was naked that would be like looking at your grandmother in her birthday suit, so they didn't stir.

They did stop in the lovely town of Sorrento, where the "Ohio Trio" bus stop drill went into effect. Bob immediately declared he was dying of thirst and started looking for anything that resembles a bar, George declared that his eyeballs were turning yellow and charged toward the town water closet, and Helena declared that she hadn't bought anything for the grandkids in at least an hour and headed for the souvenir stands, only to be waylaid by a vision of hazelnut gelato in a window and spending the money allocated for the grandkids on yet another frozen treat. Conscience stricken, she decided that the grandkids would like nothing better than a gelato spoon from Sorrento and wiped it off when done to pack in her purse.

After an admittedly excellent lunch stop in Amalfi following a four hour drive, they took the Italian Turnpike back to Pompeii, a drive that took them in a loop to where they had begun, a drive that took only 20 minutes. Pompeii was really stunning, the highlight of the trip to that point. The excavations are fascinating, the plaster casts of the incinerated people and dogs at the moment of their demise sobering. Ironically, the best excavated building was Pompeii's brothel, and their mischievous guide made us all guess before entering as to what this building might be. Since it has a marble penis projecting from the top, it's kind of obvious,but he made us yell every synonym for brothel until finally someone yelled "whorehouse" and he was satisfied. This building has the best preserved paintings in Pompeii, kind of a Kama Sutra of possible positions for slow learners.

Their enjoyment of Pompeii was marred only by a fat gent clad in purple whom Helena dubbed Barney, and to whom George grafted on the extended nickname of Barney the Weeble ("they wobble but they don't fall down"), since he always seemed to be in front of them, wheezing and sweating, and who would fart and then lurch to the side to avoid the fog, leaving them to enjoy it. They thus had a graphic demonstration of the sulfurous mist that rolled over Pompeii from Mount Vesuvius in 79 AD and killed every resident before the ashes descended on them.

Back to the ship for supper and in bed and asleep by 8:30, since they had a 5:30 AM wakeup call to do it all over again the next day.

The next morning began with a docking in Civitaveccia, the port for Rome but a 90 minute bus ride away. In Rome, their first stop was at Trevia Fountain for the ritual tossing of the coin into the fountain to assure a return to Rome. Unsentimental Bob was not going to do it, declaring that he had already scratched Italy off his Bucket List and was not coming back, but Helena shamed him into doing it. George offered him a quarter and a nickel, and he threw the nickel, which George supposed will assure Bob of a return about 100 miles off the shore of Delaware before his ass sinks into the Atlantic.

Rome traffic was not nearly as bad as they had heard, being basically a fleet of Smart Cars and motor scooters, either of which can actually be swatted out of the way by any reasonably fit American.

Helena had adopted a new persona, Wingwoman for Bob, in her quest to mate him before the trip is over. She did a good job culling one female traveler on their bus, a cutie from Boulder. George asked her what year she graduated from college, on the pretense that "our nephew had gone to Eastern Illinois University and maybe you knew him." (He actually went to Eastern MICHIGAN and is a good 10 years younger than this woman), so she blithely gave her graduation year and they quickly calculated her to be 42, within Geiser's range of preference (40-95). After Helena manipulated the lunch seating to match them up, it turned out she was a real estate agent, which gets Bob's vital bodily fluids pumping faster than any topic, so they spent the entire meal discussing square footage prices in places Bob will never even visit, much less move, and Bob evinced absolutely no interest in any of her more obvious attributes. Helping this lad is impossible.

Their second stop was the ruins of Rome, and this two hour stop was worth every penny that they spent to get there. The Roman forum was interesting, but once one steps into the Roman Coliseum, where the grandeur and savagery that occurred there for centuries can be visualized, whose size is simply mind-boggling, that was when Bob and George just shut up and stared for a good half hour. That, my friends, was worth coming halfway around the world.

Their final stop of the day was the Vatican City. The scope of St Peter's square is immense, much larger in person than one can derive from televised images, and despite a broiling sun, several metal detector scans, and 10,000 other pilgrims waiting to see the same things, the final admission into St Peter's Basilica, with its *Pieta* by Michelangelo, the tomb of St. Peter, the actual body of Pope John 23, being spruced up for beatification and on display like Lenin, and just the overwhelming space of the largest church in the world, was worth all the discomfort it took to gain entrance.

That, and the fact that lightning did not strike when Bob, George and Helena entered, made their day.

They did not get back to the ship until 10 minutes before departure, well after dinner had started. This did not deter Bob and Helena, determined not to miss a single morsel of fat-saturated food to which they were entitled. Although Bob is so anal about cleanliness he has been known to bathe between the 9th and 10th hole of a round of golf, all they did was pull one of Helena's Handi-Wipes out of her purse, wipe the grime of 2000 years of history off their hands, and head for their table. George, on the other hand, mindful of his duties to you, dear readers, retired to the galley to munch celery sticks and sip mineral water so that you, so thirsty for enlightenment, would not have to weep soft tears that another installment had taken so long to materialize.

Part 9

It was Sunday night, and they were docked in Livorno Italy, which is the port for Florence, which is actually smack in the center of Italy. Once again they had to take a 90 minute bus ride just to get to their destination city.

Helena had borrowed a book from a friendly passenger about the glories of Florence, and she intended to read up last night, but when she got to the line on the first page that said Florence has the best gelato in Italy, she started trembling so violently in bed that she couldn't read any further, so they really had no idea what they were going to see once they pried her away from the first gelato stand she encountered.

Sitting in the Celebrity Theater waiting for their tour, they were baffled by the Mexican tour arranger who kept calling for "pink stinkers" and "Jello tickets". Helena finally figured out he meant "Pink stickers" and "Yellow tickets," and they were able to board the right bus.

Fortunately, after their 8 AM departure, their first stop was the small and famous city of Pisa, home of the Leaning Tower, which by golly does indeed cant well right of center. They all took turns taking pictures at an angle which made them look like they were keeping the tower from toppling, which every tourist has done since the first daguerreotype was invented. Pisa is absolutely gorgeous, its central square easily toured in about 45 minutes, and immaculately maintained with the greenest grass they had seen in the country.

Back on the bus for another hour, they were to be dumped in Florence for four hours of "on our own" time. It now being lunch time, they sat down and had their first pizza of their entire stay in Italy. They all agreed it was very tasty, and while Bob was so agreeing he managed to dump a whole stein of beer into the lap of his white pants, so for the duration of their tour of this fine town he had to constantly hear titters, women pointing to the public water closets, and children asking mothers why they had to go in the toilet when the big bellied old man did not.

Helena rescued him from being the center of attention by spotting a store called "Paradiso del Gelato." Thinking she had died and gone to heaven, she stood drooling in the window, hopping back and forth from foot to foot in obvious agitation over only being able to choose four or five flavors for the first go-round. Then she discovered the Holy Grail, a hazelnut gelato with chunks of Cadbury chocolate in it, and after holding out a 20 Euro note and asking the countergirl how much that would buy, she was well content to cruise piazza after piazza in oblivious bliss.

Which was just fine, as every back street of Florence leads to another piazza more beautiful than the one before. On one corner is Michelangelo's *David*, on another corner is *The Rape of the Sabine Women*, on the next the tomb of Dante, on the next a palace of the Medici family. Four hours was just an appetite whetter; they did not have time to go into any buildings, and they decided to save that for the next time, when they come to Florence as the ONLY Italian city they visit.

The most fascinating was the Piazza Duomo, completely dominated by ornate churches with *faux* Moorish architecture. It was here that kind-hearted Bob encountered his next problem. The plaza was filled with "pregnant" women, whom Helena later clarified were gypsies with pillows under their blouses. They walked around in feigned discomfort, shaking a cup and begging. Pegging Bob for an easy mark, one approached rubbing her belly and pointing her finger at Geiser, saying "You my baby daddy!" Geiser, already mortified by his wet crotch, dumped all the change in his pocket in her cup and fled wildly away, only to run headlong into the path of a police car coming to scatter the gypsies. Bob immediately dropped into a linebacker stance he has not used since his coaching days in 1973, to fend off the *carabinieri* in the car; they only stopped and shook their head at this American who obviously had too much to drink, no time to find a water closet, and was sadly in need of his tour guide to take him back to the ship.

After this excitement they all agreed that sitting in the shade and waiting for their escort with a bottle of fine chianti was just the ticket.

The ride home was uneventful until they came onto the dock. Their ship is anchored right next to the Dole dock, where imported fruits arrive in Italy. At precisely the same moment, all three of them got their first glimpse of Dole's new corporate logo: a phallic banana dancing gaily, nude except for a *sombrero*. Its name, one which would become increasingly familiar in advertising campaigns and constant usage among the Monday Morning Golf Buddies, was BOBBY BANANA!

George did not have to say a word. Geiser saw the next year in brilliant foresight, and even Helena realized the import and patted a moaning Geiser on the head until they disgorged from the bus to re-enter the ship.

Tomorrow would be the French Riviera, but more importantly, LOBSTER NIGHT at dinner, and all seven tablemates will show no shame in double ordering the main course, and then sneaking back for a second seating reprise.

Our most pleasant event of the day was on their return to their room. George bought a history of the Catholic Popes yesterday in The Vatican City, and it came with a 2' by 3' poster of Pope Benedict, which he has hung on the mirror of their stateroom. Their room steward Lorna, from Mexico, constructed a little altar with candles and extra chocolates in front of it, and blesses them every time they pass her in the hall.

Part 10

This would probably be the last sea-going epistle, as they were now putt-putting toward Barcelona. It was Tuesday, an at-sea day, and they could very easily have made the leg from Villefranche to Barcelona overnight, but the cruise line needed to get rid of out-of-date milk and other foodstuffs, so they spent a day at sea barely moving, while they had a "Bavarian Buffet" composed of bratwurst (aka hot dogs no one ate), sauerkraut (spoiled cabbage and leftover cole slaw washed in brine), chicken (George noted some Central American crew members stalking sea gulls yesterday), and other detritus of the glory days of the beginning of the cruise.

George sat in the Waterfall Cafe surrounded by his favorite cast of characters: Dick and Mary of Waukesha, whose ceaseless prattle can be heard over the cafeteria din; Helena across from him, eating her favorite meal, calamari salad and chocolate-filled croissants, which she discovered too late in the cruise to prevent her gelato addiction; the Brit Brats, juvenile stowaways without parents running laps through the serving lines, abusing people with their Dickensian cockney accents and laughing fiendishly when they make people drop their plates; the Botox Queen from New Jersey staring at George's computer and asking questions in a crow-like New Yawk vernacular (George assumes without really caring that the computer screen is too small for her beady eyes to read the description of her he was at this precise second composing as she talks); the sound of the Mexican Beatles doing "You've Lost That Lovin' Feeling" wafting in from poolside while two Croatian waiters stand behind George debating whether it was Billy Idol or Billy Joel who did the original.

Yesterday was their two-country "Daily Double" shore excursion. They started the day in Nice France, but with only two hours to do the town, it was totally unmemorable. George cannot regale the reader with tales of the surly and superior French attitudes, say anything about their food, or relate a single important sight they saw. They drank no French beer, ate no French gelato, but did use a French water closet after paying the one euro tariff to a low-browed mouth-breathing Gallic lout who was technically the toilet attendant but who was occupying his time watching *Law and Order* reruns while the johns backed up. Bob and George had a speculative discussion about the possibility of his malformed child taking him to the school career fair to chat up the prestige of this job.

The view of the French Riviera was pleasing, though the beaches are not sand but rocks, much like Brighton in England, so that the nude sunbathers arose with indentations, looking like they had been sunning inside a waffle iron.

Their next bus stop was the tiny nation of Monaco, where they spent four hours and enjoyed much more than Nice. It really is a picture postcard nation, less than two square miles, where the cheapest apartment sells for five million euros. The residents are still enveloped in the cult of Grace Kelly, their beloved former queen, who died in 1982 in an automobile crash. Her visage is everywhere, and by far the busiest tourist attraction is her tomb. The Monacese are very anxious, as the heir to the throne, Prince Albert, at the age of 50 has not done his regal duty and married and fathered a son. He HAS reputedly fathered a good percentage of the general population of the nation, including a son with a circus performer who currently uses Albert's progeny as a midway barker, but the Grimaldi dynasty is in danger of dying out after 700 years. Albert was preoccupied with the Olympic Games, having appointed himself to every Monaco team since he was 16 years old, mainly in yacht races, but one memorable Winter Olympics he joined the Monaco bobsled team, which was, George thought, beaten in the first round by the infamous Jamaican team about which the movie "Cool Runnings" was made.

They took a "little train" which actually resembled the tiny locomotive that runs around the perimeter of Conneaut Lake Park, a small Pennsylvania amusement park, on a sightseeing tour. There were headphones to wear to hear the translation in 10 different languages, but George's tuning device had a loose connection, so he heard about five seconds apiece of Dutch, German, Mandarin, French, Italian, Esperanto, Navajo, a unrecognized language seemingly composed of bird chirps and guttural clicking sounds, and Chaucerian Middle English in rotating order through the entire 30 minute ride along every street of the nation. They did, however, get a long long ride on the route on which the Monaco Formula One Grand Prix is run, and the vroom-vroom sounds Banana Bob Geiser was making helped distract George from the linguistic bedlam coming from his headphones.

Last night was Lobster Night, and George was proud that not one of their table double ordered the lobster. Three of them got prime rib to go with the crustacean, making their own variation of surf and turf, but the table of eight next to them ordered a grand total of 56 lobsters, and nary a word was said by the wait staff. Their waiter, Daniela, praised their restraint and wished all her tables were so well-behaved. Their special requests had been few: unlimited baskets of brown bread, glasses of ice for J. R. Ewing, marinated herring as an appetizer for Geiser, and several courses of dessert for George.

Tonight would be packing night as they disembark in Barcelona in the morning. The porters take their suitcases at 11 PM tonight, so if one forgets to retain clean underwear for the morning, one must emerge into Spain going commando, something sure to cause an international rift.

By the way, Helena had chosen a two day extended stay in the only city in Spain in which the official language is NOT Spanish. Barcelonese people speak Catalan, a Romance language variation, so the few words of Spanish George taught Geiser, "*Quiero una senorita gorda por la noche*" (George told him it means "Could I have a beer" but actually means "I want a fat woman for the night") won't produce the desired effect.

Part 11

Your trio spent the last 48 hours in Barcelona after disembarking from the ship. Bob found a banana on his luggage the last night and confronted their old tablemates at the departure gangway. They vehemently denied doing it, and Bob will never know that his cabin steward was the Judas, having sold him out with just a minor prompt from George. Bobby Banana will live in infamy.

Their Barcelona hotel was very convenient to *Las Ramblas*, the famous four mile stretch of pedestrian walkway crammed, 24 hours a day, with flower vendors, animal sellers, mimes, food stands, and all sorts of people watchers, which they quickly became. Bob and George were in agreement that the most beautiful European women are Spanish.

They did three city tours on double decker buses and gained an appreciation of Barcelona architecture. No building resembles another, as the architects strive to outdo each other with bizarre modernistic trends. Gaudi is the most famous architect, and everyone agrees that he was a mad genius. Barcelona had two world fairs, 1888 and 1928, and the Olympics in 1992, so the Spanish basically used those events to completely demolish and rebuild sections of the city. There is very little that is "old" about Barcelona.

Their first night they determined to experience Catalan food and drink. George and Helena quickly fell under the spell of sangria, the fruity wine, and Bob sampled many Spanish beers. They also wanted to try tapas, the mini-meals of the Spanish, comprised of five or six small plates of different foods which they all shared. Reader, do not ever try tapas without first establishing the cost. They had small servings of clams, calamari in two forms, some prosciutto, and some chicken nuggets- not nearly enough to satisfy the hunger of even small children- yet they ended up paying 70 euros, about $125 American dollars. They didn't need the notorious pickpockets to relieve them of their cash – the restaurateurs did a fine job of that.

Of course, they drowned their *turista* shame in drink and gelatos. Bob actually posed with one of the street mimes, so they knew he wasn't in his right mind.

The next day they did another bus tour of the town, truly gaining more appreciation for the architecture, and then decided to take a bus trip to Montserrat, the famous mountain monastery about a hour north of Barcelona. There were only 10 passengers on the bus with an excellent guide. The bus had to climb up 2000 feet from the base of the mountain, and there are so many switchbacks that it never got over 15 mph. The view from Montserrat was spectacular, as one can see all the way to the Pyrenees and the tiny mountain country of Andorra.

Yesterday for lunch they went to a recommended restaurant named *Los Quatro Gatos*, or the Four Cats, which had a fixed price menu for 12 Euros. Helena and George both had *paiella* as the first course, a native Catalan dish of Spanish rice and seafood. Bob was less adventurous with salad. For the second course, Helena and George both chose fish, and the presentation was startling, to say the least. The cook twisted the entire fish into a circle and shoved the tail into the mouth and cooked it that way, with the skin still on, so that when it came to the table, one had to eat it while gazing into its angry dead eyes. George had a tough time with it, but Helena, who grew up eating sheep's eye soup, attacked it with much gusto.

Helena and George also downed about a gallon of white sangria, so were pretty toasted for the last few hours on the continent. One final breakfast this morning on *Las Ramblas*, and it was time to head for home.

In the Barcelona airport, they were herded to and fro into an endless succession of lines by a woman whom they named *La Fascista*. She brooked no bullshit, and all she needed was a whip to complete her character. But they were in the air at last,and would arrive home late Friday night to resume their normal life, much poorer than when they left, but glad to have done it. So, assuming all goes well (there was currently a rebellion on the plane because they are having problems with the movies, and a shrewish blonde behind them is threatening the stewardess in a shrill East Coast accent), this brings to a close this chronicle of their 2008 adventures, of which George swears every word is true.

The Beldens Go To The Caribbean, 2008

Once more the exotic and mysterious Helena Belden has lured her ever-compliant love slave George on a boat trip perilously close to the Equator, guaranteeing he will spend Christmas with a body glowing more brightly than Rudolph's nose. Once more, driven more hormonally than rationally, he has agreed. So once more you are subjected to the fastidiously accurate journal of the voyage as it happens, eight days through the Seven Circles of Hell while those back home get to bask in radiant 14 degree temperatures.

For the first time, I will NOT be sending this as it is occurring. In England we were always looking for an internet cafe, and on the European cruise we forfeited almost $40 in our internet account when we left the ship, so this time I will write it during the cruise, and then send it in several parts over several days when we return. I realize this puts me in danger, as anyone I offend can drive to my house and pound the piss out of me, but I'm also assuming the weather will be so bad that most recipients won't have anything better to do than sit around for 23 hours waiting tremblingly by their computer for the next installment.

Our traveling companions this trip are a new and varied crew. Bob Geiser, our previous stooge, plead abject poverty and begged off this trip, although he did have enough money to install a new floor in his garage that looks like an organic granola bar in texture. His job at Dick's Sporting Goods, selling unnecessary golf equipment to bored suburban housewives that he lusts after but lacks the courage to hit on, must be very satisfying, to turn down the daily visits to multiple bars where Spanish-speaking wenches ply him with dangerous libations, and from which he can be pried only with the promise of a better watering hole down the street.

No, the confederation this time is comprised of a group whose connection to each other flows though the knotty tie of having spent time in the hopeless attempt to educate the youths of Windham Ohio. The cast of characters includes Bev and Orm, who live in Garrettsville Ohio and thus are by definition eccentric (for example, there are numerous verified instances of Bev being seduced by callous cads wielding a roll of Necco Wafers, and Orm eats raw onions and capers for breakfast). The other couple on the trip is Rosalie and Brian, who own a grocery store and thus cannot be blamed for casting a cost-analysis-influenced eye on every morsel of food that is placed in front of them (Rosalie, in fact, refused to eat the first day of the trip, claiming to be excessively tired, but we all suspect that she was having baked goods airfreighted in from Ohio).

We have two solos rooming together to complete this odd octet. Linda is a virgin, never having been on a cruise before, so she was easily convinced by Brian that if she remained on the toilet in her stateroom while flushing it, her entrails would be sucked out into the Gulf Stream. Her roommate is Kathy, whose Greek husband owns an island in the Mediterranean Sea and is thus "slumming" in the Caribbean with seven peasants, but she treats us kindly and seldom rubs her superior status in our faces.

We are traveling with a group of 39 people, most of whom belong to a ski club in Warren Ohio. I believe they must have taken up the sport soon after it was invented, as we are among the few who do not use a walker (female) or wear both a belt and suspenders (male and a few ambiguous ones for whom gender is no longer apparent nor relevant). Not a great testimonial for the health benefits of skiing. As usual, we are among the youngest on the cruise, a truly tragic reality that will probably dog us until our last trip on the briny deep.

The tour director of this group is an oily 50-ish fellow named Sam, who wears his thinning hair coiffed in the style of Elvis in his coffin. He has a vaguely Hitlerian mustache. Sam is definitely the sex symbol of this entourage, judging by the harem which surrounds this small-town Lothario whenever he leaves his cabin. The din of metal walkers clashing and canes being wielded as light sabers as the women jockey for position around him is unnerving.

However, Sam is a world traveler and is a font of local knowledge. He is a master at wheedling discounts for us, and we even found out that he had accumulated so many travel points with Royal Caribbean that he was able to rebate $100 into each of our accounts with the ship's bursar. So I really don't care what he is doing with those women who use Bedazzlers on their tee shirts to try to attract his attention. Sam's okay by me.

We flew from Cleveland (where we left our car parked free for the week, one of Sam's wonderful perks). Our trip took us to Atlanta, where we had a two hour layover, and thence to San Juan Puerto Rico, two uneventful flights without a single memorable event. Brian and Rosalie flew in separately, not wanting to be seen with us before absolutely necessary. Sam had booked us into the Sheraton in Old San Juan, a very nice hotel right on the waterfront. Our room had a most unusual feature, a pair of window shutters which, when opened, revealed only the wall behind them.

There is a full gambling casino right on the first floor, but the attached restaurant is hardly four-star, an upscale McDonald's called Chicago Burger. The waterfront being somewhat detached from the rest of Old San Juan, that is where we ate soon after arrival. The hotel had given us a coupon for 10% off the bill, but our waiter, named Hiram, claimed the restaurant's computer had malfunctioned and could not issue separate checks nor deduct the rebate.

He did eventually manage the separate checks, but there was no rebate. Bev, who occasionally displays the temperament of a piranha in a school of sunfish, reamed Hiram until he returned with the correct amounts and a renewed appreciation for the ability of ex-schoolteachers to smell bullshit when it is being heaped in front of them.

We were all immensely amused by a crazy gentleman who berated everyone passing by. Since we were seated outdoors, we had a ringside seat. The entertainment value ratcheted up when a policeman pulled up on a motorcycle. The man took off his belt and began whipping a van parked on the street, which is some kind of vice infraction in Puerto Rico, as the cop began yelling more loudly than the crazy guy. This went on for the better part of an hour, and we were greatly entertained, much as we had been by similar scenes in New York City, mostly involving cabbies.

A local lass told us there was a Coldstone Creamery ice cream place around the corner, so we circumnavigated the hotel block several times with nary a sighting. Only the next day did we spot it on the corner of the block across the street, a fact the girl had omitted. We did, however, gain a good knowledge of that one block, which later proved helpful in finding the local sightseeing trolley to take a tour of Old San Juan. The trolley took basically the same route we had meandered the night before, Old San Juan being fairly compact.

After six or seven times around the same block, varied only by the age of the pedestrians jumping back on the narrow cobblestone street, we tired of this amusement and decided to go to the ship, where, after all, free food awaited. Helena went back to the room to make sure she had stolen everything, while Orm hailed a taxi on the street. We lucked into a van with a driver who had no problem gently nudging the ass of a girl slowly crossing the street while texting, an astonishing maneuver which will hopefully find its way into common practice. Two minutes later and $23 dollars poorer, we arrived at the *Serenade of the Seas*, our illogically named ship. Check-in was remarkably easy, lubricated by the offer of small free whiskey sours as we stood in line. When the server put the tray down for a moment, the Windham crew proved remarkably adroit in helping themselves to at least a half-dozen more per person, including Linda, who is very quick on the draw for a newbie.

At dinner the first night we met Mel, our waiter, from Mumbai India by way of the Catskills, as he demonstrated the comic timing of a Borscht Belt comedian. He didn't blink when Brian slipped in protruding rotting false teeth, which actually would have been indistinguishable from the dental work of the locals had this been a pub in England. The omnipresent ship photographer was equally unflappable as Brian continued to wear them in a formal picture with his wife. The lensman was similarly unfazed when Kathy and Helena snuggled close to each other for their "first picture since the civil ceremony." As we were later to discover, this was far from singular on this cruise, as Brian and Rosalie, in their effort to not associate with us, appear to have selected a cabin directly in the middle of a group of aging gay men out to claim the high seas as their turf. That should prove to be an interesting on-going story-line of the cruise.

Day 2

We have docked in Charlotte Amalie, St. Thomas Island, Virgin Islands. The ship's excursion director called our room at 5:30 AM to tell us that they had canceled the tour of the historic highlights of the island, since Helena and George were the only ones to sign up for it, which does not bode well for the rest of the trip, as we signed up for a historic tour of EVERY port of call. The excursion to the nude beach is overbooked for some reason.

So, Helena and George joined the rest of the Windhamites on a shopping trip to downtown Charlotte Amalie. The town looks picture perfect from the middle of the bay, but that must be an optical illusion caused by the torrid tropical sunlight, because it certainly is NOT so once you actually reach the town.

First, we took a "taxi" with 25 passengers in it, driven by someone whose cabbie permit listed him as Jabba d'Hutt. He dropped us off at Main Street, and before we were out of the taxi we were attacked by a horde of grasping monsters straight out of a bad zombie movie from the 1970's. These were the steerers employed by the 3,897 jewelry stores in the tiny city, trying to get you into THEIR establishment. I have not been so swarmed since the kids hawking Chiclets who accost tour buses in Mexico.

I am sure they had good prices in those duty-free, tax free stores, but since Helena has all the tanzanite she wants (none) their imploring fell on deaf ears. The others in our group were more easily seduced, so the rest of the morning they were left to their own devices under the watchful eye of Orm, who was frequently seen gazing wistfully at the $2 Bud Light stall. Helena started feeling queasy, and wanted to return to the ship, but not before being waylaid by a gentleman selling "Caoch" purses, not to be confused with "Coach," which she buys on the streets of Chinatown in NYC. Spotting a large black purse into which she claimed "I can fit all my other purses," she hemmed, hawed and haggled her way into a price that just exactly matched all the money she had pulled out of her fake Buxton, an amount which included, unfortunately, our return taxi fare. George fronted her the cab money, but took it out in trade, so to speak, upon returning to the ship.

We are less than 24 hours into the cruise, and it is becoming very apparent that heterosexuals are a distinct minority on the ship. Nowhere is this more obvious than at the mid-ship main pool. Row after row of old men with earrings wearing Speedos (I haven't seen so many of those since the last time Helena's hordes of Bavarian relatives descended on Kent). The dance class for a mid-week presentation of "In The Navy " was filled to overflowing. I'm beginning to think that Geiser must have researched this voyage a little more deeply than we did. I can't wait to watch the audience reaction at tonight's "Broadway in Review" scheduled for the theater.

Day 3

Well, if the rest of the audience reacted as we did, they were bored to tears by the Broadway Review last evening. The Broadway they reviewed was nothing like the Broadway I am familiar with.

The first 15 minutes seemed to be a resurrection of the *Big Five show,* Don Webster's predecessor to the *Upbeat Show* on Cleveland television, where at least he could feature Jeff Kutash and the Upbeat Dancers. The choreographer seemed to think wearing polyester clothes and polychromatic wigs would evoke a psychedelic era, but it was just stupid, all the more so because they had segued from a bad rendition of the rumble between the Sharks and the Jets from *West Side Story*, staged with TWO dancers. It was truly dreadful, and lifeless massacres of snippets from *Chicago, Hairspray,* and, of all abominations, *Little Shop of Horrors*, cleared half the auditorium before the end of the show,

Bev would have gotten up and left but she declared her butt had fallen asleep in the hard seat, and Linda and Kathy then admitted they had conked out, so it's hard to say who actually paid attention to the show. Bev then retired to consume the stash of beer she and Orm smuggled onto the ship yesterday, because when she came out to breakfast this morning she kept referring to Linda as Helena, which I believe was an insult to both of them.

Today we are docked at the schizophrenic island of St. Maarten, 36 square miles of tiny land mass which is divided into a Dutch half and a French half. We are anchored on the Dutch side, which is why I spelled it Maarten instead of Martin. The Dutch side traffics in dollars, the French side in Euros, which is of course why our morning tour bus dumped Kathy, Linda, Helena and George on the French side, so we can be raped by the exchange rate and come home with some useless European coins in our pockets.

Waiting on the dock for the tour bus, we got definite confirmation on the orientation of many of our fellow passengers, most of whom wear Speedos 24 hours a day. As we stood in line, 452 men (actual count) sashayed by us following a tour guide holding a sign called "The Pied Piper Tour." Their buses pulled out first, and of course when we arrived at the shopping district, they had already cornered all the good fashion buys, to the dismay of all the women. Tonight is 70's night, and we expect to see all the new clothes displayed at the Village People musical.

Our tour of the island was conducted by Jose, pronounced Joe-Zay. 6'6", a black former Marine from Houston Texas with an acquired Island lilt; he may have been the most joyous guide we have had since our river tubing adventure in Jamaica, during which our leader, Albert, fired up some of the most aromatic ganja I have ever smelled (no, he did not share, bogarting the joint shamelessly). Less than 15 minutes into today's trip, and I have digital photographic evidence of this, three amoral women from the Windham schools were begging bystanders to take their picture with Joe-Zay as they clutched various parts of his body. Apparently Sam, our tour director, has lost his allure.

In all honesty, Joe-Zay did a fantastic job, and St. Maarten contributed its own special beauty. The butterflies from Canada have migrated here in time for the blossoming of the Caribbean version of kudzu, the ubiquitous vine of the American south, and the island is literally covered with butterflies, so thick that often it appeared that there was a blizzard outside the bus. I can honestly say it is one of the most unique things I have ever witnessed. The market square in Marigot, capital of the French side, is wonderfully pressure free, with tourist tee shirts mingling with gorgeous native handicrafts, and we could easily have spent more than the 45 minutes allotted by Joe-Zay.

Dinner was quite a revelation tonight. Everything has been fine, although Orm told the sommelier the first night that we were a group of fundamentalist preachers and wives and that she needn't bother offering us alcohol. Unfortunately, she was also the one who passed out the free champagne at the captain's reception the second night, and after Orm returned time after time she deduced that he was something of a congenital liar, so now she specifically asks "The Pastor" if he has sobered up yet.

No, the revelation came from an aged blond from the Warren Ski Club (she admitted to 65 but could have been fudging up to 20 years) who heretofore had been clinging to Sam. Tonight she decided to go after younger flesh. She ordered Mel, our good-looking young Indian waiter, to sit on the chair which she had pulled out next to her.

Mel, eager to earn the mandatory tip all cruisers are blackmailed into giving at the end of the voyage, complied. Suddenly, the crone jumped on Mel's lap and began grinding her hips and licking the ear of this lad of college age. Mel bucked her off as gently as he could and beat a hasty retreat, and she chased him as fast as her skin-tight dress would allow. If you could imagine Joan Rivers or Phyllis Diller chasing Brad Pitt, it would not have been more improbable. The poor fellow is probably retching back in the tiny cabin he shares with 10 other waiters, and if he is not serving us tomorrow night, and/or there is a sudden burial at sea, we will know why.

On the other hand, if the hag is glowing tomorrow, we know Mel is going to get a whopper of a tip on Saturday.

Day 4

We have docked for the day in Antigua, the first island of our voyage that can claim to have had the British force civilization and all its concomitant splendors (slavery, genocide, etc.) on the native Carib and Amerindian tribes. Helena is a little drowsy today, having gone whole hog at the penny slot machine last night and blown $7.

George and Helena are alone today on our ritual tour of the island by bus. Kathy, Rosalie, Brian, Orm, and Bev have all gone snorkeling. In Bev's case, it's just snorking, as she refuses to actually get in the water. Helena and George do not at all understand the allure of snorkeling. If God had wanted men underwater, he would have given them gills, like the inbred denizens of Mogadore Ohio.

Kathy, who shares with George a vampirish fear of the sun, spent most of the return trip huddled in the sparse shade with a Dr. Phil wannabe and his wife. They offered to solve all of the problems she was not aware she had. Linda begged off all excursions today; we suspect a liaison with one of the belts and suspenders singles on the trip. Or with Sam, the tour director, although the mummified skiers who usually leech on to him have seemed particularly needy lately.

The tour guide for Helena and George today is Donald, a native Antiguan with perfect teeth and a charming demeanor. I say this because he had a pocket full of comp passes for free drinks halfway though the trip. Helena slammed her rum punch down in about 15 seconds and went looking for Donald to try to cadge another chit from him, but the effects of the rum were immediate enough that George was able to save her from social embarrassment by guiding her back to the bus.

Antigua is an interesting place. The actual name of the nation is Antigua and Barbuda, the second name being a sandy island about 28 miles away which no one would give a damn about except that the country's only Olympic athlete, named, I swear to God, Maverick Weatherhead, is one of 1500 people living there, so they actually combined the countries in a pathetic attempt at athletic glory. They will probably de-annex Barbuda as soon as he's too old to run any more.

We thought the housing on the island was pretty shabby until Donald told us that until a house is completed, the government cannot levy a property tax on it. So most people never actually complete construction, usually leaving one end open to the elements, much like our roof in Kent Ohio after the world's most incompetent craftsman, Ed the Roofer, used Elmer's Glue instead of nails on the shingles.

We visited several old forts, made to feel completely of-the-era by having toilets that did not flush. Only after an entire busload of people used these non-functioning toilets did we realize that the buckets of rainwater sitting outside were actually the flush mechanism. We beat a hasty retreat before anyone actually tossed a pail into the brimming bowl of offal.

The rest of the day was spent watching gay gents play tag around the pool and waiting for the Serenade Orchestra and Singers to perform songs from the Great American Songbook, Big Band style. Now, ordinarily one would expect some Cole Porter, some Hoagy Carmichael, some Rogers and Hart. But nooooooo. After waiting up until 11 PM, what George was subjected to were bizarre interpretations of "Love Train" and "Cheeseburger in Paradise. "When "Mony Mony" chugged into life, George decided that lying awake next to the atonal snorting of the sleeping Helena was indeed a viable alternative, and he swiftly departed.

Day 5

Today we are visiting Saint Lucia, and are docked in the capital city of Castries. Linda, Kathy, George and Helena are taking a "historic island tour"while the others spend three hours eating in the on-board Windjammer Cafe, laying a footer for lunch.

Our tour guide is Kerlina, an attractive San Lucian lass of about 20. She told us her name, spelled it for us, and that was pretty much the last thing she said to us for three hours, in a tour that involved absolutely no history, just riding from one small village to another, being dumped out to browse the same tee shirt stalls as in the previous village, and being told to be back after "twenty minutes of shopping." $36 apiece to be shepherded to places that make a small town flea market look like Rodeo Drive.

George knew early on the game that was being played, so the rum stands were his shopping venues of choice. He drained his first rum punch at 7:42 AM EST and was off and running. Another straight shot of rum which tasted vaguely like a barber shop tonic, followed by two local beers and some banana wine, and those who know him also know that he was thus pretty toasted by 10 AM, both in sobriety and by the 90 degree temperatures.

The last stop was a fishing village named Ance la Raye, a town where the chickens have established dominance. They are feral, belonging to no one, and we were entertained by the sight of the innumerable junkyard dogs who roamed the streets being driven underneath houses by these wicked fowl. The one street vendor who dared to be barbecuing chicken was protected by a phalanx of urchins armed with long sticks to keep the nasty peckers at bay.

On the way back to the ship (we followed EXACTLY the same road going out and coming back, to give you some idea of the breadth of our tour), we roused Kerlina from her stupor to ask if the bus could drop us off at the craft market we had seen, located about a mile from the ship. You would have thought we had asked her to stop and pick up some scabrous whores to take back to the ship for an old folks' orgy. We literally had to beg her, telling her we would jump off the bus if only it would slow just a fraction. Three of the four of us later wished Kerlina had stuck to her guns, as Helena led us, as if drawn by something in her Croatian DNA, straight to the most malodorous fish market in the world. I am used to it; Bob Geiser can testify that she did the same thing in Barcelona, but I am afraid that Kathy and Linda have lost what little respect they used to have for their teaching colleague.

Meanwhile, Orm and Brian have lost control of their wives. Bev and Rosalie decided to play Fidel Castro, and sneaked up to the cigar bar during the afternoon. Firing up giant blunts, they proceeded to turn several shades of green in a remarkably short time. After determining that we had over $100 credit in our account from canceled trips and Sam the tour director's generosity, Helena started drinking cosmopolitans before dinner, and she had no idea what she had for supper, because cosmopolitans make her lips numb. Everyone tried to ignore her when she had to eyeball every single bite to figure out what was passing into her gullet. I believe she has talked the rest of the troops into drinking cosmopolitans tomorrow so they can act like her.

Tonight's theater spectacular was execrable. The mere title, *Vibe-Ology,* sent shivers down my spine. Supposedly a guided tour through the history of rock and roll, nothing could have prepared us for a black Elvis, female Beatles, and a male Cher. And the male dancers get more exuberant by the day, realizing that they are showcasing their talents for an audience very appreciative of limber men in tights and codpieces. Bev and Orm made it though exactly two songs before bailing, Linda and Kathy fell asleep as usual, and the rest of us just watched in slack-jawed horror.

Day 6

Today is our last port of call, Barbados. Most of the Windham crew is just strolling through town in the ever-diminishing hope of finding anything different than every other shop we have seen on this trip.

Helena and George, however, took a trip with the Pied Pipers to Harrison's Cave, a very unique coral cave in the center of the island. It is the most rapidly-evolving cave on earth. The inside of the cave literally rains on the visitors, who ride through in a motorized tram, and the stalactites are lengthening in an almost time-lapse method. It was definitely different than trying to squeeze though Seneca Caverns in mid-Ohio with their grandkids this summer, where Spencer took his life in his hands by shoving George's ass through the Fat Man's Squeeze while Madison and Griffin pulled his hair and ears.

By the way, Royal Caribbean gave us a healthy rebate on that dreadful trip yesterday after George wrote a scathing letter to the Guest Services desk. It pays to bitch.

The sociology of the main-ship pool this afternoon could fill a volume of scholarly analysis. I sat in the 12th floor enclosed bar overlooking the pool, and tried to appraise the scene with the cool eye of a scientist. There were exactly three women at the pool among perhaps 150 men. The Pied Pipers have evidently realized that the cruise is soon coming to an end, and they will have to return to their mundane city lives, perhaps as bankers, stock brokers, or florists, and have begun their frenzied final attempts to pair up for the last 36 hours of the trip. It resembles final call on a Saturday night at a redneck bar when all the women with teeth have been taken already.

Aging Vincent Prices with pectoral muscles melting downward like Vincent's did in the original *House of Wax*. Sad old former athletes hunkering down in the hot tub with fifteen others, so squeezed that some had one leg in and one leg out of the tub. Limpid Andy Warhol wannabees walking back and forth like bantam roosters on a Paris catwalk. Soft fat guys relegated to the upper walking track, where they amble around like the dancing hippos in *Fantasia*, knowing full well that, even if they did succeed in culling another one from this herd to go back to their cabin with them, no bed on this ship could ever contain such a coupling of fleshy puddings.

The one sight from which one cannot look away even though one knows the picture will haunt their sleep tonight: there is a wall at the end of the pool which has become a *de facto* bar, the top surface being littered with pink, frothy drinks with umbrellas in them. Lower on the wall, facing the pool, six jets shoot water into the pool, or at least were engineered to do so. Except today, a Pied Piper in a pair of Speedos is situated precisely in front of each jet, which pulsates against their crotches, enabling them to turn around and present a suitably erect package to the consumers. One fellow keeps standing in front of the jet, turning around to check the efficacy of the treatment, and then turning back around to try another dose of this aqueous Viagra. After about 20 minutes of this, his neighbor gave him an empathetic hug and they wandered off together, succeeding through mutual failure. I have never witnessed such a human drama, not even in a backwoods South Carolina titty bar populated by unwashed bass fishermen, bad golfers, and lumpy topless dancers who jingled because patrons put quarters, not dollars, in the G-strings that had disappeared into their rolls of flesh.

Day 7

Lobster Night is one of those mythically-endowed nights, enhanced in the imagination much like a small child's run-up to Christmas. The entire day is spent with visions of 10 pound crustaceans dancing across the carpet to plunge, after a final cheery wave of their claws, into a boiling cauldron, to emerge moments later already dripping in butter. Waiters will scurry to and fro, answering croaked demands of "more, more, faster, faster", as there is no limit to the number of lobsters one is allowed. Since this is formal night, tuxedos will begin to take on the sheen of sharkskin suits as sleeves substitute for napkins in order to speed up the gobbling. Lovers will twine arms to feed each other in a shipboard re-enactment of the foreplay food scene from the movie *Tom Jones* (if you've never seen it, young Tom is unknowingly seducing and bedding his own mother).

No matter how many cruises one goes on, the Lobster Night anticipation never wanes. Even if the actual event is not even remotely like imagined.

The sad lobsters that Royal Caribbean serves up would barely register on a postal scale. It is as if they hired a boat to follow the lobster fleet, with baskets to catch the poor things that those fishermen throw overboard to let them grow into at least adolescence. Four tiny bites consumes the entirety of the meat these crawdad-sized miniatures proffer. School cafeterias provide more seafood in their notorious fish sticks.

We are now on our last sea leg homeward. Six hundred miles toward Puerto Rico, another day desperately seeking something we haven't done a dozen times already, and finishing the books which have been one's true companion. Helena read *Twilight*, which probably means I will have to take her to see the movie when we return home. Just to show you how much down time I had, I read *Perfect Beauty,* the inane true crime story of Cynthia George, of Akron's Tangier Restaurant fame, and her multitude of murderous paramours. I also finished *Will in the World*, a 500 page behemoth postulating how actual events in Shakespeare's life show up almost intact in his plays. Yeah, I know what Bob Geiser would say – stick another fork in the eye. My final tome was *True North*, a incongruous choice for a trip to the tropics, as it is about Frederick Cook and Robert Peary's competition to be the first to reach the North Pole. I guess the setting of that book is mentally preparing me for the winter wonderland of northern Ohio to which we are returning, once again via Atlanta. It is 90 degrees in Puerto Rico, and 17 in Ohio. I finished the book just as the plane touched down in a blinding snowstorm and skidded on the runway at Cleveland Hopkins airport.

The Beldens Go To Europe 2010

Oh yes they are! Four years after their epic ravaging of England, Scotland and Wales, and two years after pillaging the entire Mediterranean coast, George, Bob Geiser and Helena have once more alighted in the mother country for three weeks of alcoholic abandon.

The trip almost did not happen. Helena's mother broke her leg 18 hours before departure, and the rest of her descendants are taking shifts monitoring her condition. Then George developed a flaming red growth on the side of his right foot that appeared to be a tiny little redheaded clone.

Duly alarmed, he begged his podiatrist, with whom Helena is so in love that she once begged him to cut her a la Rocky Balboa begging Burgess Meredith in the fight against Apollo Creed, to examine his foot on one hour's notice – two hours before they had to check in at the airport. Dr. K was baffled, declaring it was either gout, cellulitis, or the ugliest damned bunion he had ever seen. Helena, sitting there, was so jealous of George being the center of bipedal attention, that she stuck out her foot and demanded that Dr. K admire her cankles, her term of endearment for her own peculiar deformity. Fortunately, Dr. K was busy writing multiple, nay, a full pad of prescriptions for George- to cover anything it might be, short of an alien burrowing out from his metatarsals – and sadly announcing that every single one of them had the unfortunate side effect of diarrhea.

Other than the anticipation of George damaging plumbing the length and breadth of the British Isles, nothing else went wrong at airport check-in, and the first leg of the flight, to Philadelphia, went off without a hitch. Except that Bob, eager to begin imbibing, ordered a round of Dortmunder Gold beers for the trio at Cleveland Hopkins at $8 apiece, and when he asked Helena for his credit card, which he had given her weeks ago to charge his room reservations in London and Paris, Helena responded with a string of slack-jawed Jerry Lewis impressions as she realized that Bob's card was sitting at her house, the one thing she had forgotten to pack. Whether Bob will have to sell his body on the streets of London just to pay for a night's lodging, and be the victim of some Jacqueline the Ripper, is something that will weigh heavy on Helena's conscience.

Our heroes sat on the tarmac of Philadelphia for a full hour as a computer specialist who looked vaguely like Kramer on *Seinfeld* tried to repair the video system of this Airbus, which refused to boot up. He finally gave up, and they had to forego the four hours of *Laverne and Shirley* reruns which they had scheduled.

Once airborne at 11 PM, Bob and George, who never sleep on planes and are used to staying up 36 hours straight on golf trips to South Carolina, where the reruns are not old television shows but rather every golf story in a beloved compatriot's repertoire for the umpteenth time, settled in with books, and Helena immediately fell asleep and began snoring, much to the distress of her seatmate, a Kim Jong-Il lookalike.

She woke up only for the gourmet meal at 3 AM. She raved about the salad, which was artfully arranged flecks of carrot on a single lettuce leaf, and traded her Play-Doh-like grain roll and a half-eaten piece of cake to George for the vague promise of Cadbury chocolate bars on demand once they landed in London. She's really easy.

Once awake, she assayed the crossword puzzle in the flight magazine but stopped because it "hurt my head." Bob, meanwhile, gave up on conversing with his shy seatmate when he deduced that the lad did not know a single word of English.

The flight itself was superb, landing at 10 AM London time. Helena announced that their hotel was a short Tube ride to Tower Station, which turned into an epic adventure since the London Subway is suffering a unique type of work stoppage where only certain stations go on strike. This necessitated hauling their 70 pounds of luggage (each) on four different train switches, and then a half-mile hike past the gallows at the Tower of London to get to their hotel. Bob, of course, made whimpering noises when they passed any pub, and George dropped his suitcase on his foot monstrosity (every single pair of shoes he brought has a 50 cent sized hole cut in the side so the little bastard growing in there can see the sights). Helena amused herself on the Tube by attempting to seduce a Czech student who had four hours in London on his way home from a student exchange in Mexico, telling him she had an idea how to usefully employ that time. He left at the first stop and they last saw him heading back to Heathrow to sit shuddering for the four hours.

Once they checked into the hotel, it was time to begin sightseeing, and Bob declared there would be no sight finer than amber grain in liquid form cascading down his parched throat, so off they marched, and succeeded in downing three pints (of cider, into George and Helena) and about double that amount of wicked ales into Bob. They are keeping a record of the names of the different brews he has inhaled, and will report that at a later date.

And, as happens on almost every trip since they became senior citizens, they were asleep by 8 PM.

Part 2

It was not a good night of sleep for your writer. First, he had to stand guard the first part of the night against hooligans who had overheard Helena casually announce loudly that she "loves to sleep naked." Fortunately she had forgotten her hotel room number or she would have added that to her cider-induced declaration.

Secondly, after midnight, when George finally tumbled into bed for the first time in 48 hours, Helena,who had been snoring loudly after taking exactly 32 seconds to fall asleep, began exhaling the detritus of her very first authentic Indian meal. The room was redolent of curry and various Punjab spices, and of course George's chronic scent allergy immediately went into overdrive, with tears and mucus soon soaking the pillowcase. So George's first night of sleep was actually spent slumped at a desk in a wooden straight-backed chair resembling a Puritan ducking stool, as far from the dragon breath as possible. Helena slept 10 hours, oblivious to the punishment she was meting out. She has promised no more Indian meals, although she was eyeing the Pakistani restaurant on the next block.

The upside of the night is that the tiny troll growing on the side of George's foot has quieted down. The exact cause is still unknown, as George is taking both antibiotics and a four-fold increase in his lifelong gout medicine. He will receive the results of his blood work by email tomorrow, which should determine which medications he can drop, too late to prevent the side-effect-whose-name-must-not-be-spoken.

A full English breakfast at the free WiFi spot consists of two eggs, three strips of meaty bacon, two dildo-shaped bangers (those with filthy minds are apprised that is the UK word for sausage), a fried Portobello mushroom cap, three triangles of fried hash browns, four pieces of toast, a fried tomato, and the one traditional element totally alien to Americans, a full serving of Heinz baked beans. A hearty meal, to say the least. George ate his with gusto, though the last forkful of beans stopped short of his mouth with the sudden realization that this was perhaps the LAST thing one who had epic, gates-of-hell flatulence should eat. Too late, both for him and the entire British populace.

The morning was spent gravitating toward Leicester Square and the TKTS booth there, where cheap tickets for West End theater matinees are sold. Faced with minimal matinee choices, the trio decided to take a chance on a new musical called *Dreamboats and Petticoats* after the ticket broker said, "Senior citizens enjoy this. It has music from your teenage years, the early 1950's." Suddenly aging a decade in a few seconds, they grabbed their walkers and told the impertinent asshole they hoped they could inch the one block to the theater before the curtain rose in four hours.

They spent the lunch hour in Covent Gardens watching street performers, drinking heavily, with Bob and George girl watching while Helena scarfed her first pasties of the trip. These pasties do not decorate the nipples of strippers, but are rather like chicken pot pies inside a Hostess fruit-pie shaped outer shell. They are also pronounced like the word "past – ie", rather than the American "paste – ie".

Bob has given his first deeply philosophic utterance of the trip: "Short skirts and no stockings are the best exercise for tired eyes."

The play turned out to be a truly joyous pastiche of about 40 early rock and roll songs from the late 50's and early 60's – nothing as late as the Beatles – cobbled together with the thinnest plot line ever seen on stage, flimsier than even *Mamma Mia*. The ambiance was kind of like *Grease* meets *Pump Boys and Dinettes*. George doubted it will ever reach America due to the toxic effect of the actors encouraging the aging audience to dance during the finale of "Let's Twist Again" seguing into "At The Hop". Several porcine women began twisting and their centrifugal momentum propelled them over the people seated in front of them, resulting in a heaving mass of sweaty flesh and orgiastic screaming which was not at all pleasant to either see or hear. Rather than help them to their feet, your heroes fled though the back doors, badly needing the help of alcohol to blot out what they had just witnessed. But all three agreed that it was one helluva entertaining way to spend the afternoon.

A good supper at a restaurant called "Mary Janes" left just enough time to get to the evening's entertainment, a reprise of their 2006 adventure tracing the trail of Jack the Ripper, where a much-too-enthusiastic narrator enumerated the eviscerated prostitutes and pickled uteruses which comprised that epic crime wave of the 1880's.

The most frightening part was when he urged the 45 travelers to crowd together in a gloomy underpass, not because it had any relevance to the mad killer, but because the people who live overhead like to "gob" on tour groups. Synonyms for "gob" are "loogie" and "snot rocket". The group became one organism for the length of that stop, as wet missiles smacked the cobblestones around them.

Bob became depressed after hearing about dead prostitutes - so many missed opportunities – so they decide to call it a night. Helena and George watched an obscene comic on TV who seemed to think at saying "Elton John" and "penis" and "ass" about once minute is topical humor, so your chronicler will now close this missive.

Part 3

The morning began on a frantic note as George and Helena awoke at 8:10 after promising to meet Bob at the free WiFi breakfast joint across the street at 8 AM. And since Bob is always 2 hours early for everything, he had to spend his time watching the working girls in short skirts and no stockings parade past his ever-hopeful but always-disappointed eyes. When the Beldens arrived at 8:45, George decided that a breakfast sandwich would suffice. However, the UK definition of a breakfast sandwich is an entire traditional meal- egg, potatoes, tomato, mushroom, bacon and baked beans – shoveled between two slices of soggy bread. Lunch would have to be postponed for quite a while.

The trio decided to go to Hyde Park corner to listen to the loonies harangue whatever crowd of hecklers they can gather with their psychotic political diatribes, usually about the evil of Americans. Getting there necessitated a 45 minute Tube ride. When they disembarked at the Tube stop, which Helena claimed was the right one, they gazed at an entirely empty small green patch. Bob exclaimed that he could now claim to have seen Hyde Park (it wasn't) and was satisfied.

So they turned around and got back on the Tube and took exactly the same 45 minute trip back to where they started. However, enough time had passed on this ludicrous mission to fill most of the morning, and it was now time to go the the south bank of the Thames, to Borough Market and a long-anticipated rendezvous with one of George's former students from 20 years ago, Becky.

They were an hour early, so of course they commenced getting sozzled. George discovered a new type of beer, Crabbie's Ginger Beer, which is like ginger ale that turns one's eyeballs inside out. Several of those later, George had forgotten what Becky looked like and was accosting every 30-something woman that passed by, to the amusement of all the babushka-clad shoppers at the Market. Finally, one of the women hugged him back, and that was how he found Becky.

Becky was an early invested employee of Yahoo.com, and the ensuing fortunes of that company have allowed her to live a life which rotates between Paris, London and San Francisco as she pursues a career in music for which she is eminently qualified. She was currently studying music theory in London during the week and living in the delightful country town of Broadway on the weekend. She was wonderfully accommodating to three elderly drunks during three hours of reminiscing, and even granted Bob absolution for a *faux pas* her sophomore year that has haunted his conscience (or what passes for a conscience in him) for two decades.

By this time, the trio had to hustle back across London Bridge and hike two miles to the hotel because none of them could calculate distance in their inebriated state, and all three had an aversion to one more Tube ride that could have landed them on the other side of London, given their inability to tell east from west any longer.

After a quick ablution to sober up, it was back on the Tube a few stops to have dinner at a pub called "The Two Bangers"(honest!) and thence to the evening entertainment, a ghost walk around old London. While waiting, Bob spotted a scoliosis-ridden hag walking on the street and exclaimed that he had never seen anyone so eccentric looking (the fact that he had indeed been checking her out says much about his current state of desperation). George told him that said crone was their tour guide, and that she was the best tour guide in London, as George and Helena had been on one of her tours years ago.

She was, in fact, a television actress of sporadic employment who dresses the part of a bloodless vampire for effect in leading the ghost walk. For some reason, the word "vampire" seemed to excite Bob, and he remained entranced for the rest of the magnificent two-hour, five mile walk, so much so that he never once begged to stop at one of the innumerable pubs they passed.

The tour having ended, one more pint of cider and beer at a pub where they were by 30 years the oldest occupants, and thence to bed. Tomorrow they leave by Chunnel for three days in Paris, so your scribe has no idea when the next message will be sent. He does not speak French, and he has no idea if the World Wide Web in Paris is available in English...

Part 4

As usually happens on these adventures, they spent Saturday morning wandering around London looking for an open breakfast joint. Finding none, George remembered that the back of the placard one hangs on the door of hotels to warn the maid that there are naked people coupling inside had a menu for a breakfast buffet precisely three floors below their rooms. It proved quite satisfactory and much cheaper than the $28 each they had spent at the Charing Cross Hotel four years ago for a meager repast that had them filling their pockets with croissants and jelly just to get near their money's worth.

They needed to buy a one day Tube pass to get to the station where they were to pick up the Eurostar to Paris. However, the Tube has no human agents on weekends, and the automatic ticket machine decided that both Helena and Bob's credit cards were maxed out despite Visa willingly extending a million dollar limit to these profligate Americans. Fortunately, Bob found a sanitation worker who was able to figure out how to trick the machine, and they were ready to head for the Continent.

Now, the very reason they were going there was because Bob has a hard-on to experience great engineering feats. The Beldens have traveled with him through the Panama Canal, where he wanted to live in Manuel Noriega's old palace, which had a never ending supply of prostitutes. They have seen the levees of New Orleans, which turned out to be rather dismal failures as engineering constructs. And for the past 10 years he has been chomping at the bit to travel through the Chunnel under the English Channel.

Quivering with anticipation, Bob and the two less impressionable Beldens boarded the Eurostar behind three very very very old women who were taking turns riding in a single wheelchair. The other 18 coaches were all loaded and ready to go while they were still waiting for these fossils to get in. Now, George has nothing against old women – hell, he's married to one – but if one is actually dead, the judicious thing would be to acknowledge it.

The Eurostar rockets across the countryside at over 100 mph with little sensation of motion. Very quickly all 60 people in their coach were lulled into a torpor, and thence to sleep.

All 60 people.

And Bob slept all the way through the Chunnel.

All the way.

With a start, he lurched awake and asked Helena why all the visible signs were in French. The ensuing crestfallen look on his face was priceless, like a little boy who has lost his first grade girlfriend.

But soon they were in Paris, city of lights, city of magic...

City of bullshit.

The Metro Subway smells like it was gang-pissed by unspayed feral tomcats. The men are unvirile and stink of stale smoke. The women BELIEVE they are beautiful, although the percentage of that is small (Barcelona women would blow them out of the boudoir) and they wear far too much perfume. It is more cosmopolitan than London, but that is hardly a selling point to Francophobes like Bob and George.

They checked into their hotel, badly in need of a bidet, only to discover that the bathroom is so small that one must sit sideways on the toilet to take a dump, making it so hard to reach down to wipe that it is hardly worth the effort, so they have ceased trying, enabling them to smell like authentic Frenchmen. The room is so tiny that the corner of the bed protrudes into the hallway. And they of course are booked into a street-fronting room that has nightclubs both below and across the street. Everything about this room spelled hell on earth for three days.

So who should take the blame for this fiasco? Groggy Bob, who wanted to come here? Helena, the internet booking whiz?

Actually, no one, because of 1-800Hotel.com, which deserves to die for what they did to the trio. Although, come to think of it, they HAVE died.

Because Helena booked the Paris rooms through them in early July, great rooms at a great price. The sonofabitches already had filed their bankruptcy papers, and still took $1200 from the Beldens' credit card. The first hint that anything was wrong was when a law firm sent Helena papers early in August so she could get in the lienholders' line to get back pennies on the dollar. Helena called the hotel in Paris and was told they had canceled the rooms on July 14.

A week from departure, Eurostar train booked, and the Beldens and Bob had no rooms.

Helena spent the next 48 hours alternating between calling Paris hotels at $5 a minute searching for a room, and calling Visa to contest the charges.

The day before they left, Visa credited her account with $1200.

Eventually Helena got rooms for the trio - at hotels a mile apart. Bob got by far the quieter hotel. So they have to designate a rendezvous spot each morning , which Bob promptly forgot, so he spent an early Sunday morning roaming the streets of Paris looking for George and Helena (although they suspected he was scouting for a courtesan). George was not at all happy, now entering his second 24 hours sans sleep.

And so they set off for a Sunday in Versailles – Louis XIV the Sun God, Marie Antoinette's bedroom, the Hall of Mirrors, the Treaty of Versailles, all of that- which was a 15 minute Metro ride from their hotel near the *Arc de Triomphe*.

If, that is, they had read the Metro map when they got in the trolley. Because if they didn't, they would end up two hours outside Paris watching country wenches milking goats and wondering where in the hell they were.

They then took two hours more to return to the Metro stop where they should have transferred, which was actually WITHIN WALKING DISTANCE OF THEIR HOTEL. They sat on an outdoor Metro bench watching the 10,000 runners in the Paris marathon shuffle by. Those harriers got to Versailles before the Beldens did.

But they had nothing better to do before leaving this Satan-cursed country, so they arrived at Versailles at about 1 PM instead of the 9 AM they had planned on.

They stood in the ticket line for a full hour, inching forward to get their admission stub. Just before it was their turn, two 50-something Scandinavian men brazenly jumped in the line right in front of them. Of course, they were too aghast to say anything that the bargers probably wouldn't understand anyway. But George, who was jotting notes in his notebook at that moment, did not take this abuse without retribution. So if one ever sees a Danish man somewhere with the word "Asshole" written in ballpoint pen on the bottom of his white jacket back, you will know who the linejumper was.

After all these teeth-grinding preliminaries, though, you, dear reader, are expecting George to say that Versailles was worth the effort. You are an idiot if you think that.

Versailles is a vision of Hell. There were truthfully almost 10,000 visitors on this sunny Sunday, and they changed the type of tickets a line was selling several times in that hour, forcing one to go stand in another line. Once you were inside, there was NO way to get out before passing through the entire palace, even if you were having a heart attack. The men's room urinals pissed back, the flushing water being crotch-directed instead of a cascade down the porcelain.

And all this to see the prize possession of the French Republic – the many and varied crappers the different Louies used, some marble, some gilded with heavy gold leaf. One even had a desk built into it so one Louis could record each evacuation he had.

What an anal country.

A much quicker trip back to Paris and many pints of alcohol later, they all hoped to flush the memory of this day. Sorry...I couldn't hold the pun...

Part 5

Today was they last full day in Paris, and finally the city had at least partially redeemed itself. It still didn't have a single stinking beer worth drinking, but Helena was happy with their wine, and Bob and George were just biding their time drinking swill until they can get back to England, which has the best beer in the world. And cider too.

They built the entire day around the HoHo. For those who have not traveled to Europe, the HoHo is the Hop On, Hop Off bus. For 29 euros they had all day, from 9 AM to 8:30 PM, to travel all around Paris on a double decker bus, jumping off whenever they wanted to visit a site.

From this base of operations on a bus 10 feet above the Paris streets, they finally discovered that Paris did have a lot of glamour. That, and it kept them above the stench emanating from French men. They toured around Notre Dame, the Bastille (where Marie Antoinette lost her head), and finally jumped off at the Louvre, where they got to see the Venus di Milo and the Mona Lisa, along with George's personal favorite, "Presumed Portrait of Gabrielle d'Estrées and Her Sister, the Duchess of Villars", a 16th century painting of two women twisting each other's nipples like they were tuning in a shortwave radio.

They saw scooters galore, thousands of them, including models with two front wheels and others which were completely enclosed with tiny cabs. They saw policemen on roller blades chasing Senegalese selling tchotchkes without license to do so. All in all, a wonderful day, but what is it with the French and their toilets? They had yet to find a toilet outside their hotel that has a seat. Do the French enjoy having their butt cheeks splash in water? And without fail every urinal but one will have duct tape and plastic covering it. The women's loos must be just as bad, because there is inevitably a line a block long whenever a toilette can even be found.

After riding the bus for 10 hours on and off, they were looking forward to being discharged by the *Arc de Triomphe,* their home base. Silly Americans. The French amuse themselves by actually meaning 8 PM when the pamphlet said the buses run until 8:30, because at the Bastille, four miles down the *Champs de Elysees* from the *Arc de Triomphe*, the driver popped his head up to the second deck and snarled the only English words he knew: "Get off. Ride done."

So Bob "Bird Legs" Geiser, Helena "Cankles" Belden, and George "There is a stillborn troll attached to the side of my foot" Belden gamely made the trek down the *Champs* toward home. Halfway there, the city lights came on so they could see where they were going. Sadly, they were also able to see that they had been tramping in horseshit courtesy of the mounted gendarmes vaguely visible in the gloom ahead of them. So now they could honestly say they smelled like Frenchmen.

They had been planning to go to a restaurant which billed itself as a British pub, but when they trooped in to look at the menu they were greeted with looks of revulsion by everyone in the room, and were told, in so many words, that they were not welcome .

Helena said that they had barged into a private party, but George thought it was the fecund odor of equine turds they had borne into that hoity-toity assemblage. Too bad. Why don't they just eat the horses that had done this to the trio's shoes - isn't that a French custom?

So they went to McDonald's and had Big Macs at midnight. It was a perfect ending to a perfect day.

God, their return to England can't come too soon.

Part 6

They had never ever been so glad to be home. Paris was a distant, rank-smelling memory, and they were back in the greatest city in the world, London, where the Tube smells of nothing worse than whatever odor a third rail gives off. They checked back into the Tower Hill Premier Inn, and found that they have been granted huge rooms, almost three times the size of the previous ones. They also have twin beds, so now Helena can gorge herself with ethnic food to her little heart's content without emitting noxious fumes in George's face all night. He loves her, but does not sleep well in a gas mask.

And needless to say, they had pints of ale and cider in front of them within minutes of check-in. No more French sheep piss that passes for beer.

(By the way, Groggy Bobby stayed awake all the way through the Chunnel this time.)

Fifteen minutes later they were back on the Tube for a trip to the British Museum. Helena managed to be a one-woman Tube gridlock, as they discovered that she has not been discarding her daily Tube pass after the last ride of the day. George and Bob passed easily through the gates (which do not whack men in the gonads, as the Paris Metro was fiendishly engineered to do) while the flustered American woman rummaged through piles of receipts, Metro passes, and old gum wrappers to find the current Tube pass she had purchased only moments before.

George and Bob harmonized on the Beatles song "Daytripper" to Helena's humiliation and the chortles of the riders who had managed to get through before this human drain clog struck. Once through, the men demanded that she hand over all extraneous paper from her pockets, since they did not trust her to dispose of it.

At the British Museum, they visited all their old favorites. Bob had a picture taken with a giant head of Ramses II, George visited the Lindow Man, who had been a human sacrifice 1200 years ago and had been tossed into a peat bog and perfectly preserved. Helena patiently viewed everything in her path, an exemplar of perfect patience, until she meekly suggested that perhaps they had seen enough and she knew a local place they could visit next.

Helena, you see, had sniffed out the only gelato shop in London.

Readers are advised to read through the chapter on the 2006 Adventures in the Mediterranean to see how this Italian ice cream gained its hold on Helena, changing her into something like those poor souls who have had angelic visitations at Lourdes and call on the Lord to take them now in their moment of rapture.

Like a bloodhound on the trail of her prey, Helena led the boys though a driving rain from Great Russell Street to Covent Gardens, until at last she stood in front of frothy, shimmering mounds of icy sugar treats. She had learned to control her whimpering and trembling long enough to stammer out the names of the gelato varieties she wanted to try this time, and for the next 15 minutes or so, only the low moaning and heavy breathing usually associated with predator phone calls were heard in her vicinity. Occasionally, she bared her teeth and snarled if anyone came close. But when she was done, she was so docile that she would go anywhere and do anything.

The trio popped back to the hotel and then out for fish and chips and alcohol in preparation for yet another ghost walk, this one starting at St Paul's Cathedral, where John Donne was the pastor and is buried. They had purchased a discount card for the London Walks so that they would only have to pay six pounds per walk, a decided bargain. If, that is, one remembers to bring the card. But Helena the Daytripper had decided to "hide it in a secret place" so it wouldn't get lost in the recycling bin she calls a purse. Do you need to be told that it was such a secret place that she couldn't find it, as the tour guide stood patiently waiting in a monsoon for this daft woman who claimed she had the discount card but somehow couldn't locate it?

They paid full price for the walk. And Bob and George have a new code word for Helena's antics: "UFB". It starts with "Un" and ends with "believeable."

The walk was as always entertaining despite the rain (it's not cold here, most days reaching almost 70 degrees). They did get wet, obviously, and were accumulating a stash of stinking clothes that eventually they won't be able to wear for the third or fourth day, and will soon have to allot time for a laundromat, which is always a high point of a European trip. Someone always spots George's giant knickers and gets all bug-eyed about it.

UFB!

Part 7

Their last day in London was about as perfect a day as any tourist could ever ask for,about 63 degrees, no more than a hint of spiderpiss mist late in the afternoon, good company, no major clusterf**ks – perfect.

They started the day late with a wonderful breakfast at their favorite restaurant, Wetherspoon's. Now, if the reader googles it, she will find it is a chain restaurant. Probably the closest USA equivalent is Applebee's or TGIF, but Wetherspoon's always chooses an old historic building suitable for rehabilitation while maintaining its original ambiance. This particular Wetherspoon's actually borders on the archaeological excavation site of a Roman cemetery. They have wonderful breakfasts for just over three pounds, and many supper plates which always include a pint of one's favorite alcohol. George paid 16 Euros for a burger and fries in Paris; here, a burger, fries and a pint are less than six pounds, less than one would even pay in the USA.

After breakfast, they set out by Tube for Westminster Abbey, the fifth visit there by George and Helena, and it never gets old. Seeing Elizabeth I and Bloody Mary buried in the same tomb, standing next to the tomb of Geoffrey Chaucer, walking on the grave of Charles Darwin, tracing the history of England by the tombs and memorials dating back to before the Tudor monarchs – priceless.

Unfortunately, they were chased from the Abbey after only half a tour because the BBC had taken it over in preparation for the Pope conducting a service there on Friday. Who would ever have believed the Pope in the lair of the arch-enemy Anglican church? He was having a service in Hyde Park Saturday, and later in Manchester and Edinburgh. The Beldens thus had to schedule their touring to avoid him. And the BBC was all aflame since the Pope's right hand man actually called England a third world country yesterday.

For lunch, Helena and Bob discovered the wonderful world of Sainbury's, a food chain that has the world's greatest selection of prepared foods as well as groceries. Helena chose a prawn and arugula sandwich, while Bob bought a one pound slab of Cadbury chocolate. Yes, Helena has a convert to her shameful hidden vice of hammering chocolate bars into her mouth pretty much any time of the day.

At two PM they began a three hour walking tour of Beatles sites in London associated with the Fab Four. Amazingly, they had scheduled this event the same day Paul McCartney arrived back from a tour. The guide pointed out that Paul's 3rd floor office, to which only Paul has access, had a light on, and damned if that famous head didn't suddenly appear in the window. Helena, who has no luck at all, had wandered to another spot to get a picture of a quaint hovel, and as George and Bob screamed for her to get over there with her camera, the famous head disappeared. Of course, Helena called Bob and George goddamned liars but another American couple confirmed it. The only thing that prevented a crying fit was that Helena was always hot for Ringo Starr.

Bob let slip that they were going to Liverpool to continue their Beatles quest, and two pretty young girls on the tour begged to join the trip. But the boys needed Helena along as a navigator, so they had to turn the luminous college-age girls away. Helena vowed to repay them for even thinking of tossing her out. She got her revenge before the end of the day.

They took a Tube train three stops to Abbey Road, where Bobby, ever solicitous of the safety of the women in the group, stood directing traffic so that all could get their pictures in the famous crosswalk from the cover of the *Abbey Road* album. Helena signed the wall in front of the Abbey Road studio, which is whitewashed once a month and where messages to the Beatles are encouraged.

After the conclusion of the tour, they chose a pub near the Houses of Parliament, where some of the best action of the trip occurred. Helena was sent outside to secure a table while George and Bob brought pints. When they emerged with the glasses, they found Helena deep in flirtatious small talk with two very handsome young men. The boys assumed she was getting directions to their next stop, but the nature of her discussion became very clear when she looked up and in a husky voice barked, "Go away." Your heroes had to wait a full five minutes until she finished fluttering her eyelashes at the lads, and then threw a withering glance at Bob and George which told them they could finally approach.

Helena had her revenge for them lusting after coeds – or so they thought,

But what happened next made that all seem insignificant. They were sitting drinking near the back entrance to the Parliament, on a side street, when, not five feet from them, the street erupted with TV cameramen and female reporters with BBC microphones. Behind the gates, maybe 20 yards from the Beldens, a bevy of dark suited men sprinted for a Mercedes and jumped in. It came barreling toward them, the gate flew open, and the car raced up the alley, hitting one of the cameramen, and then sped off. George asked another videographer who it was, and he said only two letters: "BP".

(Watching the BBC that night they saw exactly what they had witnessed: Tony Hayward, the disgraced "I want my life back" chairman of eco-violator British Petroleum, had just endured a lengthy grilling by the entire House of Commons, and it was he whom we had seen whisked away violently in that car.)

After this excitement, they agreed they needed another pint to collect themselves, so they migrated down to Charing Cross station to one of their favorite pubs from the last trip, the *Sherlock Holmes*. Helena wanted a picture of the boys sitting under the Sherlock Holmes sign, and as she made them pose, a very pretty six-foot tall 30-ish woman watched with an amused smile. George immediately went into top wingman form, smiling back and telling Bob to signal her to come over and be treated a pint, at which point George and Helena would go for a stroll. But Helena, with a nasty chuckle last heard in *The Exorcist*, told Bob he had absolutely no chance and she wasn't moving her tired ass for any exercise in futility.

UFB – one never knows the depths of this woman's vindictiveness.

Tomorrow they would get their rental car at Heathrow and leave for a week and a half of aimless but wonderful wanderings though small villages, embracing the history of this country wherever they find it.

That, and drinking whenever possible.

Part 8

Picking up the car at Heathrow went off without a hitch, the smoothest rental they had ever done. The car was a Volkswagen Passat Diesel with the steering wheel on the wrong side, but George just shifts into British mode and five minutes later feels very much at ease, as long as Bob and Helena keep chanting "keep to the left!"

Of course, it didn't take long until bizarre things started occurring. They were driving on the M25 superhighway, permissible speed up to 100 mph, when completely out of nowhere a roll of toilet paper came bounding into their lane and immediately leaped onto the grill of their car. Within seconds it started unrolling, streaming over the windshield and roof, flapping back and shedding leaves all over the cars behind them. Helena took a picture to confirm that this is the gospel truth.

Then they came up on a slower vehicle moving about 75 mph with people sitting on it. As they passed it, they were astounded to see that it was a tank rolling along on its tracks at that speed. They spent about 15 minutes skirting an area resembling an American army base, and every mile or so was posted a tank crossing sign.

Their visit to Stonehenge was the best ever, as the Brits have now added free audio guides to the admission cost. They had brilliant narration as they circled the entire area. The only negative was the enormous number of jackdaws which scream like fingernails on blackboards.

They then drove to Amesbury, where the Beatles filmed much of the movie *Help*, and where Helena and Bob once had a lamb dinner they declared was magnificent. They even saved the bones and sucked on them for the next 48 hours as they drove.

As soon as George parked in Amesbury, Helena took off like a scalded cat, sprinting for the restaurant, only to emit a high pitched scream when she discovered that lamb roast was no longer on the menu. The sight of a grown woman crying in a small village street was like something from a bad Victorian novel. George had to placate her by taking her to a Flower Festival at a local church, in which people competed in the most intricate arrangements of two or three flowers. There must have been something more than what they saw, because each of the entries just looked like, well, like a couple of flowers sitting on a bench. They didn't stay around to see who won.

Their next stop was Avebury, which is pretty much like Stonehenge except the hundreds of stones are a mile in circumference and encircle the village. It's not as instantly dramatic as Stonehenge, but they wondered why they had never heard of it during their previous trips.

Then they backtracked (using a GPS instead of an atlas has deprived them of the perspective of a"larger picture", so they have determined to use an atlas map each evening to give them the lay of the land for their next day), through Amesbury to their inn, the Lancer House, which was the first place the Beldens had stayed 20 years earlier. It no longer has an attached pub, but instead has morphed into a lovely bed and breakfast pretty much in the middle of nowhere.

They had to drive about eight miles for dinner, which precluded George from getting tanked that night. They ate at the Barford Inn, a wonderful 16th century tavern near the town of Wilton, where Helena and Bob finally got the lamb they had pined for all day. They decided to start this ravaging of Britain's sheep starting at the ass end, and they each had rump roast. George and Helena then shared a crème brulee that was so good they ended up shoving each other's spoons out of the way.

The Barford Inn sponsors a cricket team which is called "The Barfs." It actually says that on their uniforms.

Part 9

The Lancer was quite nice but different than when they had stayed there 20 years ago. No longer is it a pub where George got so drunk he offered to buy drinks for all the locals, until the barkeep announced that the large American man was a loony and not to believe a thing he said. Helena was very relieved at that, although their sons Sam and Garth, as teenagers, were looking forward to slipping into the drink line.

The Lancer is located directly across from some WWI era chalk carvings done by bored soldiers. They are called the Fovant Badges, which one can find on Wikipedia.

Before retiring, Helena declared she wanted to go to St. Ives (you know, the "I met a man with seven wives" town). George quickly replied that he would be neutered before he drove down to Land's End and Tintagel Helena countered that she wanted to go to Cornwall again and St. Ives was the Cornwall town she wanted to visit. George said "F**k no." Bob said he was scared of both of them and refused to commit to either side. So they went to St. Ives.

It was a long drive - four hours to get there at 1 PM, and for the first time in her life Helena was right. What a wonderful little seaside resort. It was staging a music festival, so the town was packed and any thought of staying in the area was banished, but that really didn't matter. Helena was in pig heaven: St. Ives turned out to be the home of Cornish Pasties, her favorite food that isn't chocolate, cider or gelato. She ran from shop to shop salivating on the windows, but refused to commit until she had drained two pints of cider, getting giddy drunk and rubbing up against a young barkeep, cooing in her boozy voice, "Hey big boy, where can a lady get a good pastie around here?" He blurted out the name of a store while retreating as fast as he could, and damned if it didn't turn out to be her Holy Grail. She bought two different kind of pasties and embarrassed Bob and George by wolfing them with alternating bites as she walked blindly though the crowd, all the while narrating how incredibly good they were and spewing pastry crust all over bystanders. One thing one can say is that the woman loves her food.

Back on the A30 with their sights set on finding a place short of Cheddar and Bath to hole up for the night, Bob detected the distinct smell of cow patties in the air and declared that this would be a good place to sleep. The inn he chose was directly in front of a stockyard, the largest in East Cornwall. As Helena and Bob booked rooms, they made George park the VW next door to the inn in a car repair yard that resembled the best of rural West Virginia, with mutant chickens jumping on the car and pecking at him through the window.

The inn, however, is a sojourner's dream. Late Victorian, it is a pub called the Wilsey Down, located in Hallworthy just outside of Camelford in Cornwall. Over the pub there are about a dozen rooms, gorgeously remodeled and very large. So they were able to exercise their favorite activity, drinking several pints (Bob had five in the three hours since they arrived, plus several smaller glasses the publican gave him as a kind of beer tasting) while chatting with the locals. Helena and George have both become enamored of a local cider called Rattler, which after a few glasses Helena slurred into Rattlesnake and eventually into "gimme another one of those serpent tongues."

The food was superb. Helena ate so many pasties during the day that she could only slurp a great potato and leek soup. Bob had a huge steak with trimmings and lemon meringue pie, and George had an amazing macaroni bake made with cheese created in this very town, and a sticky toffee cake for dessert that had him licking the dish afterward. And those mutant chickens that accosted George would furnish the free-range eggs they would have for breakfast.

Part 10

What an incredible day! Their first leg was a drive to Cheddar Gorge, one of the great natural formations in the UK. It is sort of a mini-Grand Canyon, filled with caves and the rock climbing center of England. The most interesting thing was that JRR Tolkien was enamored of the area, and that many of the descriptions in *Lord of the Rings* are based on geological formations in Cheddar. One cave, in fact, became Gollum's Cave in the *Trilogy*. They also tasted several authentic Cheddar cheeses, and bought a package to nibble on the road. The Cheddarites have a peculiar way of telling one to consume it soon: the package is labeled "Eat Me Now," which label George pried off and taped to Helena's back .

From there they went to Bath, from which the promiscuous Wife of Bath in the *Canterbury Tales* came. Bob got excited when George told him that, anticipating the streets to be teeming with trollops just lying about, waiting for this legendary cocksman from the USA. Hope does spring eternal. But it was more of a treat for Helena, as there was a Jane Austen festival going on. Hundreds of people dressed in Victorian garb milled in the streets. Helena felt faint at the sight of a Mr. Darcy and had to be kept from checking him for a codpiece. George found a toffee bar and was too engrossed in gluttony to care where her hands wandered.

They found that they had a few more hours before their nightly desperate search for lodgings, so they pulled a name from their list of the ten most beautiful English villages, and the closest was the quaintly named Castle Combe. The first entrance to the village was a road no more than six feet wide, and George refused to drive more than 100 yards before backing out and saying that his ass couldn't fit through that opening, let alone a car. But Helena whined that there must be another way in and she wanted to see it and SHE HAD TO PEE! So they drove about a mile down the road where another sign pointed the way. A very slightly wider road led in, and after about two miles a uniformed security guard stopped them and said the road to the village was closed, but they could walk the last mile if they wanted to. And he told them why the village was closed.

Steven Spielberg has taken over the village for the filming of his next movie, *The War Horse*. And the trio could walk through the sets, since filming didn't begin for two days (it's Saturday).

The film crew had converted this frozen in time Cotswold village into the year 1914. They trucked in tons of sand and gravel to cover the tarmac road and make it look unpaved. They glued moss all over the place to make it feel even more archaic. One scene will revolve around a draft lottery, and the tiny town square has been transformed into the place where lots will be drawn.

UFB!

And the best was yet to come. After sharing a pint with the locals and extras, as they hiked up the hill the mile to their car, who should come driving past them but Spielberg himself. Apparently he had no room in the movie for a fat old man, a drunk with skinny legs and too many chins, and a beautiful but weathered senior citizen lady, as he did not stop and ask them to star.

That's why they love these trips- they never know what is around the next corner.

They found an inn for the night whose claim to fame was hosting Queen Elizabeth when she was stranded in a blizzard in 1981, and Bob actually had her room. It's the closest he's had to a woman in his bed in a looooong time.

Part 11

Last night they had a sumptuous dinner. Bob and Helena of course had lamb. They had started with a rump roast two nights before, and they decided to slide down from the ass to the lamb shank listed on the menu. They were mortified when they were told that the last lamb dinner had been sold, and Helena shrieked, "Well, just go kill another one. We saw some just up the road." The chef actually came out from the kitchen and said he had some but would have to defrost it. Helena said she'd wait all goddamn night and he'd better hop to it. Of course many pints had to be consumed before it arrived. Helena and Bob both declared it was well worth the wait and that they could still probably get a couple hours sleep before breakfast.

George had chicken.

Today they left for the Lake District, a four hour drive on M6. M's are superhighways, where everybody chooses a lane of comfort and stays there, pulling out only to pass and then getting right back in. No sawing off, no staying in a faster lane and pissing people off. George has hit 90 mph and been passed like he was standing still. A's are fast single lanes which turn into dual carriage ways on hills for passing. The speed limit seems to be about 60 mph on them, and slower speeds are clearly marked on the road surface. B's are the old Roman roads, very narrow and scary. One just has to be very cautious on them. And yes, everything is backward left to right, which is why George is terrified to be in the car without a navigator. Between the three sets of eyes, everything has gone smoothly so far – knock on wood.

This, sadly, turned out to be a dismal day, the worst weather they had ever had in England, unfortunate in that they had chosen this day to go to the most beautiful part of the country, the Lake District. The day started out with a soft mist, and by the time they had gone an hour on the M6 they were flashing flood warnings on roadside signs. It never really rained that hard, but if one can imagine the road spray coming up from three lanes traveling 75-90 mph, that was the hellish thing. And it was a four hour drive, truly nasty.

They drove through Ambleside and Windermere, towns Helena and George had visited before, and motored to Hawkshead, the town that Beatrix Potter worked out of. The drive to Hawkshead was 15 miles of B roads that were barely wide enough for two cars, let alone touring buses. There were the ubiquitous stone walls towering about seven feet high less than a foot from the passenger side of the car. Helena and Bob stared at the rocks well within arms reach and sounded like two mourning doves with their incessant "ooh" and "no no no" whines, punctuated by an occasional "oh shit" from Bob the useless tourist. Nary a drop of sweat was seen on the brow of the consummate driver.

From Hawkshead they went to Kendal, a larger town but supposedly just as beautiful. The rain persisted, though, and the wonder of the town went to waste. But one good thing did happen (George had found a quid on the ground and was due some luck, and since neither Helena or Bob fell in Lake Windermere to lessen his psychic torment, it had to be something else).

It was – he found a discount bookstore, and since they were traveling blind, with nary a guidebook in the car, he thought he'd just check to see if anything like that was in the racks. Lo and behold, there it was: for two pounds, a guide to the best pubs and inns in the UK, a dream for a drunkard like Bob, a godsend for someone who cares more about lodging, like George. He found an inn listed in Lancashire, less than half an hour from tomorrow's destination of Liverpool. Helena logged it into the GPS, and they were delivered to a wonderful ancient hostelry called the Farmers Arms. George and Helena had a suite for 55 pounds, and Bob had a very nice single for 35 pounds, the least they have ever paid. They ate in the pub below, drinking and deciding on what the meal will be – undoubtedly another lamb stolen from a grieving ewe for the mastication pleasure of these two gustatory monsters.

Helena decided to be nice to George for this wonderful discovery. Perhaps she meant she will sleep on the couch so he won't lie awake all night listening to the symphony of snorts, whistles and belching noises she makes all night long.

At dinner, the lamb butchers were again presented with a multitude of choices. One of them was noisettes of lamb, which logic dictated were probably the vocal cords, ripped out so the helpless things couldn't bleat while other parts were chopped off them. Alas, they instead both chose lamb steaks, which were so huge three serving wenches had to carry in each platter. They not only ate the entire things, they poured the excess bloody juice into the finger bowls and demanded pieces of cake to sop it up with.

George had fish.

Absolutely the best news they received is that there is a launderette less than two minutes from here, and George gets to wash the pants he has worn every single day since departure 13 days ago. They have taken on a life of their own and last night he caught them carousing in the pub, ordering drinks for everyone. Bob, who brought 22 shirts with him, many of which say "I'm Horny" on the front, has run out already.

Interlude – Bob's new beers:

Wychcraft
Strong in the Arm
Black Sheep
Vecks Vier
Greene King
Badger
Spitfire
Caledonia Autumn Red
Younger's Scotch Bitters

Part 12

The launderette turned out to be a dry cleaner, so the Beldens were still hauling a trunk full of dirty clothes. They were mentally calculating things like if anyone would notice if they didn't have shirts on, or if they could handle going commando, wet wedgies be damned. And Helena declared that her pert and perky twins have been hankering for a whiff of Scottish air, so she's okay too.

The tour of Liverpool was carried off well. They had been told that the ferry across the Mersey is the ONLY way to come into town. What the bastards didn't tell them was that they had to drive 50 miles out of the way to get to the Birkenhead peninsula from whence it departs, and that just driving into town would have saved an hour both going and departing. But they did it – ferried cross the Mersey – but of course not without incident. Getting to the ticket office was no problem. The problem was when the ticket taker, with an incomprehensible Liverpudlian accent, told Helena there would be no ferry today because of mechanical difficulties. The expression on Helena's face was beyond crestfallen. Bob said that she looked like someone spit in her beer, and Helena moped, "I'd still drink that beer, but I can't swim a goddamned river."

Fortunately, the mechanical problem was repaired and they were able to depart with only a slight delay, so Helena was able to dry her tears. The ferry is actually more like a tourist version of the Miller Ferry to Put-In-Bay in Ohio – a loudspeaker narration of the history of the ferry and important landmarks of the Liverpool skyline were a real bonus.

The first thing they saw when they landed was a Hop On Hop Off, so they took a tour of the city, and to George's amazement, it turned out to be a gorgeous place (actually a UNESCO Heritage city) with lots of fantastic sights, rather than the drab dockland and industrial city it was in the 1960's.

Then came the highlight of Helena's trip, the visit to the Liverpool Beatles Museum, with artifacts dating back to the Lad's childhood days. It follows a chronology with their music from each era playing in each gallery, and is a great place for someone who knew the Beatles only through their songs. Since George taught the history of the Beatles academically for over 20 years, it seemed rather familiar and he was slightly disappointed that he got more out of the London Beatles walk than a visit to Liverpool. But it was still fun and he was glad they finally got the courage to go into the city.

Bob bought a Beatles money clip (this says SO much about his character). George had no idea why Bob bought a money clip since he has given every cent of his entire fortune to the upkeep of the Bartenders Pension Fund of England.

The trio has taken up residence in the town of Carlisle, just south of the Scottish border, and tomorrow they make their run to St Andrews, where Bob refuses to play golf because it is much more amenable to George's bump and run style of play, and Bob is tired of getting thrashed by Fatty this summer.

Part 13

George loved the inn in Carlisle, since it was the first time in a week that he had a separate bed from Helena. It was so soft and nice, and since he took the double and made her take the twin, he had plenty of room to roll around without going flesh on flesh.

Poor Bob didn't fare so well. The only other open room was the one that they had designed for handicapped people, of which he is one though not in the legal sense. The mirrors and sink were at the height someone in a wheelchair could use , but which Bob could only use by getting on his knees. When he was shaving, he looked like a druid worshiping a porcelain god. There was also a string hanging from the ceiling which he assumed was the light. It wasn't – it was the alarm siren that a disabled person in distress would pull. Leave it to Bob to turn a good night's sleep into a Keystone Kops routine.

They had a three hour drive through the Scottish Highlands to reach St. Andrews, and the first half of the drive was through a fog so thick they couldn't see 50 yards in front of them, on two lane A and B roads. George, who is self-admittedly a brilliant driver, had absolutely no problems, and Bob and Helena could not see that they were 900 feet in the air clinging to mountainsides on roads where horseshoe curves were the norm. So George did not have to put up with their perpetual whimpering and baby noises.

It was really worth the drive. The sheer joy to walk down the fairways of the place where the game of golf was born is exhilarating. They walked across the famous stone bridge on the 18th fairway, taking each other's pictures. They saw the 17th green, where the stone wall is in play and often a billiards shot backward is the only shot. They hid behind the shed that juts out into the 17th fairway and where players have to take a blind shot over the hotel name on its wall to be anywhere near inbounds. They even got to see a player's shot end up on the asphalt road that crosses the 18th, and he had to play it from there, as there is no relief as from an American cartpath. In other words, a real highlight of two golfers' lives.

Helena shopped.

The drive back was taken over the same roads, and Helena and Bob were horrified to see what George had driven in the fog. The aghast looks on their faces made George laugh so hard he almost did go over a precipice.

Tonight was the first time they have done the "no room in the manger" routine. They deliberately chose inns in the real backwaters of northern England, places no sane person would drive to, and got turned away from the first three places they stopped. Finally, it was getting dark, and George does not drive in the dark, and he was hungry and is a real prick when he is hungry, so they chose a Premier Inn just off the M Roadway. The irony is that it is in Carlisle – they drove a 250 mile loop today.

Tomorrow they are looking for Hadrian's Wall, going to York, one of their favorite cities, and finishing with an attempt to close a genealogical void in George's heritage.

And they hope that the appearance of three haggard Americans who STILL have not found a launderette doesn't cause innkeepers to call each other with warnings.

Part 14

It was the best of times, it was the worst of times. From 7 AM until 6 PM it was a wonderful Wednesday. They ate breakfast at McDonald's, and discovered that their free WiFi is the same company that services Wetherspoon's, so they had automatic log-on to get the internet.

From thence they went in search of Hadrian's Wall. After a bracing walk across the moors, they found it and shot some wonderful photos of the Roman equivalent of the Great Wall of China, built 2000 years ago across the entire British island, 85 miles long, for the sole purpose of keeping the Picts imprisoned in Scotland. The Picts, history records, regarded Roman flesh the way Bob and Helena regard sheep – objects to be devoured on sight.

And following the time-honored tradition of golfers everywhere, and being many miles from a loo, Bob and George, both of whom take diuretics, peed on the wall as a form of territorial marking.

From the Wall to York was a three hour drive on A and B roads that offered George the most invigorating driving of the trip. Having a car with tight cornering (which is, incidentally, getting 50 mpg) is such a treat. Every once in a while, a golden pheasant would fly up right in front of the car, eliciting "holy shits" from everyone, and several times they had to stop quickly because a sheep was standing in the road. Helena kept urging George to hit one and throw it in the trunk for a midnight snack.

York is such a magnificent walled Roman town, with slices of history relating to the Vikings, Anglo-Saxons, the War of the Roses (remember, the Yorks vs. Lancasters), and pretty much every monarch for the last 1000 years. After London, it is their favorite city, and this was their third trip. Their first move was to ride the HoHo and get a real sense of the city. As they strolled the streets, there was a Taste of Yorkshire food festival, and Helena almost wet herself at all the choices. She ended up with a Yorkshire pastie (naturally), Bob had a sausage roll, and George had a flapjack, which is basically a granola bar which has been drenched in syrup and then half-dehydrated. They had pints at a 1503 pub called the Golden Fleece, which of course had a lamb on the pub sign which hypnotized the sheep-savaging twins.

From York they started a leisurely drive to an inn we had stayed at 20 years ago near Haworth, home of Emily Bronte of *Wuthering Heights* fame. Apparently the name Belden has lingered in local lore for two decades, because they were unceremoniously told to get out. That became the first of nearly a dozen rejections – and it was getting hear dark, and George has never driven after dark in the UK. They kept missing turns in the roundabouts, and Fiona, the name we have given to the British female voice of our GPS, was actually calling them stupid bastards. Helena kept telling George to ignore Fiona, earning her the new nickname of Helena Overrider. Inevitably, Helena's choices ended up disastrously, but since George needs her alive to care for him in his dotage, he refrained from killing her.

Finally, a kindly innkeeper took the time to call around and booked them into an ETAP Hotel, a chain based in France.

Another reason to hate the goddamned French.

This hotel is the most spartan place in which they have ever stayed. It literally looks like a prison cell at Alcatraz. There are no electrical outlets, one towel, and there are teenage trollops circling the parking lot. Bob, of course, eyeballed them with a grin, but Helena convinced him that spending the money for the return trans-Atlantic trip on something as ephemeral as a five-minute tryst was not in his best interest.

So he said that if he couldn't have sex he could at least have the cigarette he would have had AFTER sex, and went to the Tesco supermarket and bought a pack of cigarettes and a lighter. He went outside to light up and couldn't figure out how to get a flame from the English-style lighter. He asked a security guard to show him how to do it, but pathetic Bob could not duplicate the intricate motion required. A seven year old boy then showed him, but Bob, try as he might, could not produce a flame, and he was getting red in the face, as only Bob can get. Finally, he asked the clerk to take it back – at which point another clerk said they had lighters for the handicapped in the back, which even quadriplegics can operate. It still took Bob about five minutes, but he finally fired up and immediately began hacking his lungs out and smiling. It takes so little to make him happy.

Interlude

More of Bob's beers:

Jennings Cocker Hoop
Kinder Downfall
Centurion Ghost Ale
Chatsworth Gold
Carling
Copper Dragon Black Gold
Muldoon's Black Adder

Part 15

The ETAP hotel was even worse than they imagined. Once they pulled back the bedspread, the bed itself was a sheet of plywood on legs with a two inch thick mattress on it. George did not sleep a bit on this morgue slab, great prep for driving in the Peaks District.

Dinner was Big Macs at McDonald's, and on the stroll over, on a darkened street, Helena caught a couple in a car engaged in what the English call "anti-social behavior." For once in his life, George will refrain from further description, but Helena claims the bloke was more interested in looking at her than the slut beneath him.

But as dawn broke and George blearily watched his ninth hour of BBC News which had absolutely no relevance to him, the day took a turn for the better.

After breakfast at the same McDonald's, they took off for a small nearby town called Baildon. One must say the name out loud to realize why they went there. According to George's brother Deane, the family genealogist, the Belden family came from Baildon several centuries ago, with their family taking its name from there. Deane had asked them to visit Baildon, and they did.

And they were amazed at the connection between the town and the Beldens. The largest church is the Methodist Church (all the Beldens except George are Methodists; George worships the pagan Saint Helena). The main social club is the Liberal Club.

172

The clincher is that the village center, in the only roundabout in the village, still has its original stocks and whipping post. So now they knew WHY the rascally Baildons came to America.

But the greatest proof that they were home was that, as they toured the town buying every souvenir they could find, they stumbled upon the finest sight to greet their eyes in many a day – a launderette.

Knickers, bras, shirts worn five consecutive days – all came pouring out as they commandeered EVERY washer in the place. They were now ready to go to Heathrow without fear of the drug dogs mistaking their stench for home brew methamphetamine.

And they even found their lodgings by 1 PM in a wonderful old inn called the Devonshire Arms in the tiny town of Forest Peak, which they used as a base to explore the Peaks District. First stop was their favorite village, Bakewell, which the Beldens strolled for the third time. It is the quintessential English market town, with a wonderful shallow river rolling through town. They debated going to visit a cave with the delightful name of The Devil's Arse, but after all the baked bean breakfasts they decided that it had nothing on them. Even Mount St. Helena erupts with Old Faithful regularity.

Their final stop was the town of Chesterfield, which has the most bizarre church spire in the world. Looming over the town, it was built of unseasoned wood, rather than stone, and over the 400 years since it was built, it has twisted around upon itself like the top of a Dairy Queen cone. The town legend is that a virgin once got married in the church, and the spire twisted around to get a look because it had never seen a virgin in a local wedding.

They also became criminals in Chesterfield, as George put their paid parking sticker upside down on the dashboard, and Lovely Rita the meter maid, who had her knickers in a bind, decided that such a heinous act was worthy of a 50 pound ($75) ticket. They did plan to protest the ticket officially, although, since the traffic magistrate is the Sheriff of Nottingham (really!), they're not sure he won't decide to hang them instead.

Or whip them in Baildon.

The Devonshire Arms was an old stagecoach inn which a postman for the Royal Mail bought and refurbished for himself and his wife. The trio were the only ones there. Helena had lamb cutlets for dinner, which George believes are cut from the belly, leaving a hole in the lamb for the rest of its short sad life. Bob had liver, his second favorite dish; George swears Bob is the only person on earth who enjoys it.

George had salad.

Their room on the third floor had a cathedral ceiling with a fireplace and skylight. Unfortunately, the bed was tucked into the eave end of the room, so whenever George sat up in bed he whacked his forehead. In the morning, they awoke to the sound of a howling Yorkshire wind, rain, and a 30 degree drop in temperature. And Helena had chosen this Friday to be market day, a tour of Staffordshire market towns.

They almost didn't make it, because 15 minutes after leaving the inn, Bob began complaining of a sharp pain in his ass. Since he once had a hemorrhoidectomy, he knows his pains in the ass. But it turned out to be his room key, a 300 year old skeleton key actually, which he had forgotten to turn in. Helena immediately began flapping her hands frantically and declared that she too still had her room key. George, of course, was completely innocent as these two senile twits claim he can't be trusted with anything important. They drove back to re-deliver the keys, putting them quite a bit behind in their day's activities, but George, as is his wont, was patient and kind.

Their first market town was Leek, where George and Bob had their picture taken under the sign of the main pub, the Cock Inn. Helena refused to reciprocate with a picture that George could send to her quilt guild. Leek had a very nice market, but the only thing they bought was some cough drops for Bob, who now has developed a mysterious dry cough. They also had blueberry and menthol drops but Bob thought the combination too bizarre. George bought some treacle, for which he has developed an affinity, much like Helena and her Cadbury chocolate. She is seldom without a chunk of chocolate melting in her mouth, and she speaks in what the boys call the "chocolate voice," which sound like someone coming from the dentist after having her wisdom teeth removed.

On leaving Leek, they drove by about the tenth "cattery" they had seen. Bob believes they are brothels, but Helena assures him its just a hotel for kittens.

The next town was Cheadle, which has a strange dildo-shaped whipping post still erect in the middle of the town, apparently used to punish wayward women in some incomprehensible fashion. Helena did not mind posing next to it with a Mona Lisa smile on her face. George discovered a new regional treat, oatcakes, which are actually like blintzes.

The next planned stop was the town of Nasby, from whence their good friend Linda Thompson had discovered her great-great-great grandmother emigrated. They were going to take pictures for her of the town sign and town hall.

They never made it.

In the next installment, the reader will find out why they were now driving a BMW instead of a VW, and what it feels like to be hit in the rear by a British lorry.

Part 16

Yes, you heard right. The Beldens had a car wreck bad enough to put them in another vehicle.

They had set their sights on Nasby, and were driving down the A50. George has driven through 10,000 roundabouts in his life. He went through at least 100 that very day. But this roundabout was different – a massive amount of traffic moving through a circle connecting a huge motorway – and all the lane markings had been worn off the pavement. If one is going around a roundabout – and they were going 270 degrees around this one – one can ride the left hand lane all the way around, maintaining the right of way...

Except in this roundabout, the TWO outermost lanes were allowed to exit at 90 degrees, a fact that had been worn off the pavement markings. So as George entered the roundabout in the left hand lane, a huge lorry, hauling either grain or cement, entered in the right hand lane, and as George continued around the circle, the lorry turned into the 90 degree exit – right into the driver side of the VW at about 30 mph.

George saw it in the rear view mirror as it was about to happen. Bob felt the contact and had time to get an "oh no" out. But the entire crash took about one and a half seconds.

The lorry crumpled the driver side back door, about six inches behind the driver's seat door. It wasn't a horrible crash, and actually more of a gentle push that started the VW pinwheeling through the roundabout. They were not sure if they did a 540 degree spin or a 900 degree spin, but the Volkswagen ended up on the grassy outside of the circle facing the oncoming traffic.

They were fortunate to end up there, as they were not in a direct line of traffic flow. No air bags popped, but they all sat stunned for at least two minutes while regaining their senses. The lorry driver pulled over down the road, and worked his way through traffic to get to them.

His first concern was their health, and after they had checked all their parts, they began to pull everything together. The lorry driver said, "You're Americans? You have a saying, 'Shit happens.'" And that was the best thing they had heard in England.

His name was Patrick, and he was the nicest person one could ever meet. His truck only had a few scratches, and he pulled out a set of forms and began his job duty of filling out a report. Since there were no injuries, no police report was needed. He called the Recovery Assistance Corporation, the national service that rescues all wrecked cars. He also called Sixt, the Beldens' rental agency, and then Bob took over and arranged for the car to be towed to the closest VW agency. Patrick left, and they then stood in the roundabout for an hour waiting for the tow, with nary a policeman passing by.

Richard, the RAC tow operator, took them to the Stoke on Trent VW agency, and he then waited around to contact Sixt for more directions, which took about half an hour of calling and waiting. He went way beyond the call of duty.

Sixt told them they would arrange for another car to be delivered to the VW agency. The people at the VW place gave them coffee, soft drinks, use of their phones, and became their hosts for four hours while they waited for Sixt to arrange with Eurocar via National Rentals for a BMW to be delivered to them for the rest of the tour. Since the car did not arrive till 6:30, they decided to stay in the Holiday Inn just 100 meters away.

They drank heavily that evening.

George will never enter a roundabout again without holding his breath.

They decided that their last two days would be spent wandering within 50 miles of Heathrow airport. They spent most of Saturday in Oxford riding the HoHo and buying golf shirts with the Oxford University logo on them. They then drove through the Cotswolds doing their usual "where are we going to sleep tonight" and chanced upon an ancient hostelry in the town of Deddington, which has four pubs. They drank in all four before dinner. They decided that tomorrow they will book a Holiday Inn in Maidenhead, only a 20 minute drive from Heathrow, early in the morning, and then do a tad more meandering.

New beers:

Adams "The Bitter"
Hook Norton Copper Ale
Hook Norton "Hooky Bitter"
Windsor Guardsman.

Part 17

They drove an hour from Deddington to Maidenhead, with just a few rhetorical questions by the men about how that name could have been derived. They checked into the Holiday Inn Maidenhead at 11 AM, and the tariff was 133 pounds, more than they even paid in London. They would have told the shysters to forget it at that price (the rooms are tiny and they don't even have free WiFi or free breakfast) but did not feel like trying to find a place in what is essentially a bedroom community.

They had the entire afternoon for their final English experience, so they had to choose between Windsor Castle and Hampton Court. Helena and George had been to Windsor Castle in 1990 (and were thrown out for filming Henry the Eighth's grave), so it was off to Hampton Court.

And what a brilliant choice it was. It was the main homes of both Henry VIII and William and Mary, with the W&M part added long after Henry died. They were basically given free reign with audio tours, and were most impressed by William and Mary's state apartments and bedrooms. The best part of the Henry tour was through his kitchens, where they saw how dinners were prepared in 1540 for 600 guests a night. Modern cooks could have no conception of the amount of labor and the hundreds and hundreds of people, from supply clerks to piemakers, necessary for the meals to arrive and be satisfactory to a notoriously temperamental king.

Henry had 60 different "homes" in England, and he never stayed in one home for long. The guide said that it was because after a while, so many meals had been prepared, and so much offal had accumulated that the homes and castles began to stink horribly, so he would move on to the next one. Helena thought it was because he had pillaged all the available virgins in the area, sowing his seed prolifically and leaving ugly little Henrys everywhere.

Period interpreters roamed the castle, and one was liable to bump into Henry anywhere. The trio all had their picture taken with him, and they chatted about which one of his wives was the best banger. They also toured the 65 acres of gardens which were planted by Capability Brown, who is the god of gardening, to those of us who have pursued that frustrating occupation.

Bob and Helena, for once, were on their best behavior and did nothing at all worth reporting. They did not eat lamb for dinner, since eco-terrorist texts from PETA have begun appearing on Helena's phone.

They settled into the bar at the Holiday Inn, and anticipate a 7 AM wakeup call and a 20 minute trip to Heathrow. They had some settling up to do with the car rental agency – exactly what to do about the wreck, did they have any speed camera tickets (although George NEVER drove faster than surrounding cars, and was very careful on A and B roads, one never knows what the cameras saw until the end of the trip).

But of course it couldn't work out that well. After a harrowing trip to return the BMW, and Sixt telling them the exact opposite of what Sixt had told them on Friday – to bring the car to them – they tried to get George to drive to the other side of Heathrow to return the car to Eurocar. A loud "No fooking way" from both Bob and George convinced them that George was done driving and they could take care of the car themselves. And there were no speeding camera tickets waiting for them, either.

The actual flight from England was fine – tons of entertainment which they could choose individually – and the landing was perfect. Until, of course, Helena turned on her cell phone and found a call from US Airways telling her that their flight from Philadelphia to Cleveland had been canceled. A series of calls got them booked on a flight an hour earlier – exactly one hour after touch down from England. And they still had to go through Customs, and TWO security checks. The final indignity was that three fat 60 year olds had to sprint a half-mile through the Philadelphia airport to arrive at the desk just as final boarding was called. As one incompetent desk clerk searched for any verification that they had been placed on that flight, another incompetent clerk was calling up standbys to take the Belden seats. One quick "Don't you dare give away our goddamned seats" from George put a stop to that nonsense. They were all seated in different parts of the plane, but they made it to Cleveland when they hoped to.

Their luggage didn't.

Bob's soiled underwear, Helena's souvenirs and George's pill box (almost two dozen a day) arrived at their homes days later. And THAT, finally, brought a successful conclusion to the triumphant 2010 European tour of George Belden, Helena Belden, and Bob Geiser.

[And by the way, George has never driven in England after drinking. He knows their laws: driving while "unfit through drink" carries a maximum penalty of six months imprisonment and a fine of up to 5000 pounds.]

45045392R10103

Made in the USA
Middletown, DE
23 June 2017